The *201* Questions Every Homebuyer and Homeseller Must Ask!

Edith Lank

Real Estate
Education Company
a division of Dearborn Financial Publishing, Inc.

Acquisitions Editor: Christine Litavsky
Managing Editor: Jack Kiburz
Associate Project Editor: Stephanie C. Schmidt
Interior Design: Lucy Jenkins
Cover Design: Design Alliance, Inc.

96 97 98 10 9 8 7 6 5 4 3 2 1

Library of Congress Cataloging-in-Publication Data

Lank, Edith.
    The 201 questions every homebuyer and homseller must ask / Edith
Lank.
      p. cm.
    Includes index.
    ISBN 0-7931-1434-9 (pbk.)
    1. House buying—United States. 2. House selling—United States.
I. Title.
HD259.L36 1996   95-9131
333.33'83—dc20   CIP

Contents

Part Two   Homeselling

P*reface*

Over the years, I've sent tens of thousands of personal letters to readers who sent in questions to my syndicated real estate column—and lately I've also been answering queries that come in by e-mail.

I hear from investors, landlords, tenants, brokers, bankers, even lawyers, but mostly—

- from buyers and sellers.
- from you.

So here they are, the answers to your most frequently asked questions about buying and selling a home.

They're arranged to carry you through the whole transaction, from your first decision to move, right down to your dealings with the IRS after it's all over.

And if you still have a question when you're finished reading, I'd love to hear from you—and I'll answer.

—Edith Lank
240 Hemingway Dr.
Rochester, NY 14620

e-mail to lank@sjfc.edu

Chapter 1

*E*xploring the Homebuying Process

*T*here are better and worse times to be a seller, but it's almost always a good time to buy.

If your local market is down (a buyers' market), sellers will welcome you with open arms, and you can do some bottom-fishing to pick up a bargain.

If the market is hot (a sellers' market), you're well advised to get in as soon as you can and share in the growth, even if you can't yet afford your dream home. Otherwise, the house you want to own eventually will go up in price faster than you can save money toward a down payment. In such a market, buy whatever you can, as soon as you can.

Before you start to look for a home, you may be interested in a few facts about the average buyer in the 1990s. Recent surveys show that about half of all homes are sold to first-time buyers, whose median household income is roughly $53,000—but remember, "median" means half of these first-time buyers earned less than that figure.

Only 44 percent of homebuying households are made up of a married couple with dependents. One homebuyer in four is single, and many unrelated persons are buying homes together.

Home sales, then, are about evenly divided between first-timers and repeat buyers, whose median household income is about $60,000.

Aiding these changes are new ideas in financing. Your grandfather was probably offered a simple mortgage at a standard fixed interest rate, but today you can choose among hundreds of innovative plans, each designed to meet the borrower's particular financial needs. Of particular value are special financing opportunities developed in the mid-1990s designed to help first-time buyers get into the market.

1. How does owning compare with renting?

A retreat from the pressures of an increasingly crowded society, the need for self-expression, inflation, tax considerations: all enter into the decision to buy a home. When you own your own home, you can play the stereo at midnight, keep a dog (keep *two* dogs!), make a garden, drive nails in the walls wherever you want and use your own washer and dryer.

No one can give you notice to move.

Your property taxes and interest payments are deductible on your income tax return, and the portion of your monthly mortgage payment that goes to reduce the principal debt acts as automatic enforced savings.

If, on the other hand, you will be in town for only a year or two, it's not likely you'll come out ahead buying and then selling a home. The concept of homebuying as a quick and simple sure-fire investment died with the 1980s.

If you presently have an unusually good rental at a very low figure, you might prefer entering the real estate market by buying a small investment property.

You may have a demanding job, with little time left for the maintenance required of a homeowner. Or you may not have any desire or aptitude for the constant demands of real property. Many people take creative satisfaction in mundane tasks like hosing down a garage or trimming a hedge, but if you're the type who would have to call a plumber every time a faucet washer needed replacing, you might find home ownership more of a burden than a joy.

If you travel often, you may feel easier about leaving an apartment, without having to worry about lawn care, snow shoveling or a vacant home while you're away. In that situation, though, consider buying a condominium, which combines some of the carefree aspects of an apartment with the financial advantages of home ownership.

2. I'd like to buy, but I may be transferred soon. What's my wisest move?

If you think you may be selling within a few years, you can protect yourself by buying carefully. You want a home that will appeal to the widest possible group of potential buyers down the line. Even if you need only two bedrooms, buy a home with three and, if possible, with two baths—the most popular configuration today.

Avoid anything unique or highly personalized. A tract house in an area with young families and some turnover is probably your most prudent bet. Buy the least expensive house in which you can feel comfortable; that way, there will be more people who can afford it when you're ready to sell.

3. Can I afford to buy?

It takes just three things to buy a house: some cash, dependable income and good credit. And if you lack any of these three, no need to despair. Home ownership is still possible. There are techniques for overcoming each problem.

Just be sure to level with the real estate agent you work with about your financial problems. A competent agent can recommend an appropriate financing strategy for your particular situation.

In the 1990s, home ownership offers one of the few remaining tax shelters. Property taxes on one's home and even on vacation property are completely deductible. Interest paid on up to $1 million worth of borrowing to acquire or improve a home (or two homes) is deductible—and that more than covers most of us. If the value of your property rises over the years, additional borrowing of up to $100,000 in equity loans, refinancing or second mortgages also qualifies for federal tax deduction.

Depending on your tax bracket, you'll find that Uncle Sam, in effect, makes a certain percentage of your monthly payment, with deductible property taxes and interest forming almost the whole payment in the first few years of the loan. The government's contribution will show up in the form of lower income tax owed or unexpected income tax refunds. Further savings can be expected on state income taxes.

In addition, profit you make when you sell your own primary residence qualifies for several delightful income tax breaks. If you replace your home with another of equal or greater value within two years (before or after the sale of the first), tax on your profit is postponed indefinitely.

You can repeat this process any number of times, piling up untaxed profits on a string of homes. Then, any time after you reach age 55 or older, you can take advantage of a one-time chance (you choose when to use it) to sell your long-time home and take up to $125,000 in profit free of any federal income tax ever. And that exclusion can include untaxed profit on previous homes.

4. What is equity?

Besides the tax saving, in most areas you can expect some increase in the value of your home, an additional return on your investment known as *equity* buildup. Localities vary; brokers can estimate what might happen in your area over the next few years. If you could conservatively expect the value of a home to increase by $3,000 in the next year, that might justify up to $250 a month more in mortgage payment.

Equity represents the amount you'd have if you sold your home and paid off the *liens* (financial claims) against it—usually, the mortgage. If you buy a $120,000 home with $25,000 down and a $95,000 mortgage, your equity, the day after you move in, is $25,000. Equity is the money you've got invested in the home—it's like money in the bank.

If the house goes up in value by 5 percent in the next year, and your debt is paid down *(amortized)* by a paltry $1,900 that first year, your equity has grown to $32,900 (market value, $126,000, less remaining debt, $93,100).

Equity buildup assumes, of course, that the value of real estate goes up.

Not since the 1930s have real estate prices varied so much from one area to another as they do now. At any given time, one part of the country sees rising values while another is hit by unfavorable economic factors. The real estate market is cyclical: a drop in prices eventually attracts new industries and turns into recovery. At one point, the farm states are badly hit, but prices skyrocket on the East and West coasts; then the Midwest sees steady growth and increase in values while the coasts experience what stock analysts would call a "correction."

Overall, the United States experiences gradual growth in real estate prices every year, at least matching general inflation. Many experts believe that the major problems affecting certain areas—factors like unemployment, drought and fluctuations in farm prices or the price of oil—have already been discounted, with the severe drops behind us. And in hard-hit areas, it's great to be a buyer. It's like buying stocks at the bottom of the market; recovery is almost certain.

5. What's my first step?

To prepare for your purchase:

- Start reading classified ads in the real estate section of your newspaper. Visit open houses on the weekends—all this even though you're not yet ready to buy. The more familiar you are with areas you might want to live in, the better off you'll be when you do act.
- If you're a veteran, send for your VA certificate of entitlement, just in case you end up wanting a VA mortgage.
- Contact a credit bureau, and pull a report on yourself, just to make sure no mistakes will turn up (they do in many accounts). One of the major agencies, TRW, will send you a free report on yourself as often as once a year; call it at 1-800-682-7654. This is particularly important if you've had credit problems in the past. It pays to start clearing things up early.
- Sock away extra cash. You'll be motivated to skip a vacation or a movie when you have a short-term goal like accumulating money for down payment and closing costs.
- Don't buy anything on credit. This is not the time to take on another car payment, buy a boat or even apply for an additional credit card.
- If someone will make a large cash gift toward your purchase, get it into your own savings account months before you apply for a mortgage loan.
- Apply at a lending institution for preapproved credit. If, down the line, a seller knows you are assured of the mortgage loan you need, your offer will be much more attractive and perhaps even worth a price concession.

Chapter 2

*L*earning about Those Agents

*A*s you begin your house hunting, it helps to keep straight the various terms describing real estate licensees.

Agent is a general term for anyone empowered to act for another. Agents owe a special set of legal (fiduciary) duties to the persons who hired them (their clients, or principals). More on that all-important point later in this chapter.

Broker is a legal term for someone licensed by the state to negotiate real estate transactions and to charge for services.

A *salesperson* holds an entry-level state license, allowing that person to assist one specific broker, somewhat in the position of an apprentice. The broker is legally responsible for the salesperson's activities. (In some areas, the word *agent* may be used to describe a salesperson, as opposed to a broker.) A salesperson may not operate without supervision and may not collect any fees except from the sponsoring broker, usually as a share of commissions earned by the salesperson's efforts.

REALTOR® is a trademarked designation (properly capitalized, like Xerox or Frigidaire or Coke) used by a broker (in some areas, a salesperson) who belongs to a private organization called the local association or board of REALTORS® and also to state and national associations. REALTORS® subscribe to a code of ethics that goes beyond state license law and often sponsor a local multiple-listing system that offers access to homes listed for sale by many different firms.

REALTOR-ASSOCIATE® is the term used by some boards of REALTORS® for salespersons associated with member brokers.

So, as you start your search for the best agent, decide whether you prefer a salesperson or a broker. There's something to be said for each. In general, you can expect a broker to have more education and experience. On the other hand, some long-time salespersons remain in that status simply because they prefer not to go into business for themselves. And you could run into a well-trained, highly motivated newcomer with the time and enthusiasm to do a first-class job for you.

6. Does it matter who the broker works for?

So you think you're looking for "your" broker! In recent years, a study by the Federal Trade Commission found that most buyers believed the agents who helped them buy their homes were their agents, putting the buyers' interests first. Many sellers also thought so, and, regrettably, so did many brokers.

It just ain't so. If you walk into a car dealership, you don't assume the salesperson works solely for your benefit, do you?

The Law of Agency clearly sets out the broker's duties to the principal (also known as the *client*), the one who retains and (usually) pays the agent. These fiduciary duties are complex, but they boil down to one main point: the agent must put the principal's interest first, above anyone else's, including the agent's own concerns.

Many states have passed laws in recent years requiring that you receive written disclosure of agency. You may be asked to sign an acknowledgement that you know which side the agent works for. Don't sign the notice without reading it. And consider how it will affect your purchase.

7. Do you mean I have to learn about Law of Agency?

Absolutely. You need to understand an agent's fiduciary duties, which include the following:

- *Obedience* to the principal's instructions unless they are illegal. (Examples of instructions a seller's agent would not obey include "Don't show the house to any Lithuanians" and "Keep quiet about the broken furnace.")
- Loyalty to the principal, which, strictly followed (it sometimes isn't) means the seller's agent should obtain the highest possible price for the property and never suggest any offer less than the listed price.
- *Confidentiality,* which prohibits the seller's agent from sharing with you details of the seller's financial or family situation unless, of course, the client has authorized such action (for example, running an ad that says "Facing foreclosure, seller desperate—make offer!"). Whether the seller received previous offers, and for how much, would also be confidential information.
- *Notice,* a duty that obliges the seller's agent to forward to the principal any fact that would be in the seller's interest to know. *This is of vital importance to you.*

Unless you specifically hire your own buyer's broker to represent you (more on that later), none of these duties is owed to you. Even if you work with a different firm than the one that listed the property, both firms are agents for the seller. The second one, *the one you're working with* (let's not say "your agent"), may be a subagent of the first firm and of the seller. You are merely a third party in that relationship, a customer rather than a client.

8. Where do I stand as a buyer?

It can be scary to realize you are merely a customer, but things aren't as bad as they seem.

First, the law does require the broker to be honest, straightforward and trustworthy with third parties. Your questions should receive honest answers, although sometimes an honest answer might be, "I can't answer that; I must keep the seller's financial information confidential."

Besides answering your questions honestly, agents and sellers have an obligation to volunteer information about any serious (material) hidden defects you could not see for yourself. State laws differ, though, on whether they must also tell you about *stigmas,* past problems that don't technically affect the real estate, like suicide or murder on the premises, illness of the seller and the like.

Next, you will receive a great deal of service paid for by the seller because, without this service to buyers, the property might never be sold.

Finally, you can take heart from the fact that, as a practical matter, many brokers violate their duty to the seller. A good agent empathizes with you, wants you to find what you want at a price you can afford, may emotionally adopt you. If brokers didn't to some extent identify with buyers, not much real estate would get sold!

9. How do I protect my interests?

If the agent is duty-bound to put the seller's interest first (and there's only one first place), how should this affect your relationship with a seller's broker?

First, realize that no confidentiality is owed to you. It's only practical to reveal your financial situation if you expect to get effective service, but you may want to keep some information to yourself. The broker who knows you would pay more "if we have to" is—strictly speaking—obliged to convey that information to the seller. Saying "but don't tell the seller" won't help because the agent does not have any special obligation of obedience to you. Never say anything to the seller's agent that you wouldn't say to the seller. Assume that whatever you say will be (or at least should be) passed on.

Take advantage of the fact that you should receive honest answers to your questions. In some states, you are entitled to a seller's written disclosure of defects, but elsewhere, "Are you aware of any defects in this home?" is a good all-purpose query to ask of both seller and broker, preferably in front of witnesses.

10. Can I hire my own broker, one who will put my interests first?

You certainly can.

Until a few years ago, buyers' brokers were used only for the purchase of commercial property. Today, however, buyer representation is offered by many firms and is often used for simple residential purchases.

If you want to find an agent who operates as a buyer's broker, call a few of the largest real estate firms in town and speak with the managing brokers. If a company does not offer the service, it should know which ones do. Often a lawyer who is active in real estate can give you the names of buyers' brokers. You may also find brokers who advertise their specialty in the yellow pages.

The buyer's agent may ask for a nominal retainer to compensate for time invested; sometimes the retainer applies against eventual commission due or even against the purchase price of the property bought. If no property is bought within the contracted time, the retainer may be forfeited.

Occasionally, the buyer pays the usual share (perhaps half) of commission originally promised a selling broker when the house was listed for sale. In return, the seller may reduce the sales price by that amount because the seller will pay only half of a full commission to the listing broker.

In theory, the buyer who specifically hires a broker should pay for the service. In real life, though, it usually works out that the seller pays the originally agreed-upon commission, part of which goes to the buyer's broker.

Why would the seller be willing to do that?

To help get the house sold.

Buyers, first-timers especially, don't have much spare cash lying around when their sales close. Just to make the deals work, sellers are often willing to furnish the commission in that fashion. In the same way, sellers sometimes pay the "points" charged by banks (more on that in Chapter 8) just to help buyers obtain mortgage loans.

Proponents of the buyer's broker system like it because it sets up an adversary situation similar to that in which the parties retain two different attorneys. Sellers and buyers each have a broker clearly working for them alone, without the conflicts of interest that can arise under the more traditional system.

If you hire your own broker, expect to sign a contract in which you promise that during a specified period of time, you will not house hunt with anyone else and that if you buy any property within that time in any fashion, your broker will be entitled to a fee.

The system can work well. A buyer's broker is committed to helping you negotiate the lowest possible price, is free to point out drawbacks in any particular property and must keep your information confidential.

A problem can arise, though, if you find yourself tied to an agent who does not, in the end, suit your needs. But it helps to remember that the old-fashioned method, in which you would deal entirely with sellers' brokers, has been around for years and can also bring satisfactory results.

11. Is it ever a good idea to buy from a FSBO?

Sellers who handle their own property are known as FSBOs (pronounced "fizzbos" or "for sale by owners"). Some do it for the satisfaction of tackling an unaccustomed job, not to pass on the saved commission to you. They usually plan to sell at fair market value and pocket the commission as extra profit in return for their efforts.

You will have extra work when you buy directly from an owner. Unless you retain your own broker, you'll have to negotiate face to face, obtain additional attorney's input into the written contract, explore financing options on your own and ride herd on your own mortgage application process. It may be extra important to have your own building inspector look over the property before you commit to the purchase.

You may want to buy from a FSBO if the place is unique—exactly what you want and haven't been able to find in listed properties. And sometimes you will run into a home that has been underpriced by a FSBO who chose to do without the services of an appraiser as well. In that situation, be prepared to act promptly; some investors lie in wait for unwary FSBOs and jump as soon as underpriced property hits the market.

Otherwise, it is usually a waste of energy to start your house hunting with FSBOs. Until you have a good grasp on prices in the area and the entire homebuying process, it can be difficult to deal with homeowners who often have exaggerated ideas of their homes' value and who don't know how to proceed. Wait until you, at least, know what you're doing.

Chapter 3

*F*inding and Working with the Best Agent

*I*f you're moving to a new town, write to the chamber of commerce there asking for maps and information. Alert brokers often subscribe to the chamber's inquiry list, and you will probably hear from several brokerage firms interested in working with out-of-towners.

It's always a good idea to subscribe to local newspapers before you move to the new locale. Not only will you get a feeling for the community and for the character of various neighborhoods, but you can see, in the classified ads, which agents are active in the areas you like.

As with your search for the ideal dentist, plumber or lawyer, recommendations from friends who have had good experiences may be the best way to find a good real estate agent. One caution, though: brokers specialize. You want someone who concentrates on the areas you're looking at or the type of house you're looking for.

Failing any recommendations that pan out, you will meet sellers' agents by answering advertisements, calling the phone numbers on lawn signs and visiting open houses. You can keep searching until you find someone who seems just right—see the question following on how to pick a good one.

12. What legal obligation do I have to a seller's broker?

None.

You might be tempted to play the field, thinking that you'll get many people out there looking for your dream home. In reality, though, the buyer who works with many brokers works with no one. The first time an agent calls to tell you about a house that just came on the market and hears, "As a matter of fact, we saw that one with someone else this morning," your name is crossed off the list. In the absence of a legal relationship, many successful transactions flow from informal cooperation between buyer and broker. If you plan to use sellers' brokers, when you find a good one, stick with him or her.

13. How do I judge whether a broker is right for me?

Apply a few tests:

- Does the agent return phone calls promptly? This simple question is a good screening device, whether you're looking for an agent or a TV repairman or a physician.
- Does the agent explain things so you can understand them? This is especially important for first-time buyers. If you can find an agent who is a born teacher, you're in luck. (Actually, in fact, many brokers are former teachers.)
- Does the agent seem ready to invest time in you? When the broker holds open a house that's on the market, for example, does he or she just wave you through, asking as you leave whether you're interested in the house and letting it go at that? You want someone who, if not busy with other prospects, shows you the house in a professional manner, asks questions about your needs and wants

and offers to sit down and discuss other places on the market if you're not interested in this one.

- Does the broker suggest an initial session in the office, rather than simply meeting you at the house you called about? To get good service, you need a financial analysis and discussion of your whole situation.
- Does the agent ask questions about your finances soon after meeting you? This may not be good manners in ordinary society, but it's the mark of an efficient broker who aims to give you good service.
- Does the broker alert you that he or she is acting as a seller's agent? (In most states, this information must be given to you in writing upon first contact.)
- Do the first houses suggested show that the broker has been listening and understands your wants and needs? If you're shown houses with the wrong number of bedrooms, or clearly out of your price range, forget it.
- Does the agent seem conversant with local conditions? Does he or she have maps of the area, handouts about schools, museums and property tax rates, and the like?

Once you find a broker with whom you feel comfortable, one who inspires confidence, stick with him or her. Tell the broker about other firms' ads that interest you, even about FSBOs, so that the agent can investigate and report back to you. Ask for advice before visiting open houses on your own. If you have the agent's home phone number, don't hesitate to use it. Real estate agents are accustomed to evening and weekend calls. Service is the only thing they have to sell, and they welcome any sign that you intend to utilize it.

14. If I have a good agent, do I need a lawyer?

Customs in real estate vary tremendously from one area to another, and in some locations you may be told that no one uses a lawyer; legal work is handled by special escrow or title companies. The law does not require that you have legal counsel. It is, nevertheless, usually foolish to proceed without professional help—your own attorney, entirely on your side. Lawyers are useful not so much for getting you out of trouble as for heading off trouble before it starts.

Your attorney will make sure the sales contract protects your interests, intervene if problems arise before closing and review final figures to make sure you get proper credit at settlement time.

Lawyers specialize, just as physicians do. You wouldn't go to a gynecologist for a sprained knee; neither do you want a corporate lawyer or a trial attorney for your home purchase. (In small towns, of course, most lawyers are generalists who handle real estate, among many other matters.)

To find a specialist, you can ask a broker to suggest two or three names. Agents know which attorneys are active in this field.

In a strange town, you might call a bank and ask what firm handles its real estate work. Or you can call a large law firm and inquire which partner specializes in real estate.

Contact a lawyer early on. Call an attorney's office, and explain that you're starting to house hunt. If you don't feel comfortable with what you hear, shop around. And never hesitate to ask what the service is likely to cost.

Your lawyer will suggest the right time for further contact. If you have financial problems (judgments, etc.) that need clearing up, you may want legal input immediately. Otherwise, you may not need to contact the lawyer again until you are ready to make a written offer to purchase a specific property.

15. What do I need the agent for, besides seeing houses?

The average person assumes that a real estate agent's job is to help you find a home, but that's only the tip of the iceberg. The typical broker will spend more time bringing you into agreement with the seller and, most important, helping you arrange to finance your purchase.

Some services you can expect—even if, as is most usual, you use the seller's broker—follow:

- *Analysis of your financial situation.* Don't be offended by what appear to be personal questions. A good agent asks them at the beginning of the house-hunting process because a lending institution will ask them later. During a first conversation, the broker is already forming a strategy for financing your purchase, based on the various mortgage options outlined in Chapter 8.

- *Education in basic real estate principles.* Brokers expect to spend extra time with first-time homebuyers. You have a right to insist that every step be explained so that you feel comfortable with it.

- *Recommendation of a specific price range.* Without those parameters, all of you—seller, agent and yourself—are just spinning your wheels. It's useful to be told the price range for which you can qualify, but remember there's no need to reveal at this point the top price you're ready to pay.

- *Orientation to a new community.* If you are moving out of town, send for the local newspaper, read the ads and write to a couple of real estate firms that handle property in the area or price range you might be interested in. You may receive long-distance phone calls, maps and offers to meet your plane, make motel reservations and arrange baby-sitting services. Seeing the town with a broker as your chauffeur is one of the best ways to learn about neighborhoods, schools, shopping and the like.

- *Information about different locations.* The agent will not answer questions or volunteer information touching on any of the classes protected under human rights law—the ethnic or racial composition of neighborhoods, for example. But a broker may answer your questions about the location of vegetarian restaurants and health clubs, give you factual information on per-pupil expenditure in various school districts and pinpoint on a map the organizations or religious institutions you inquire about.

- *Screening of listings.* The agent will show you any house that's on the market and must be careful not to narrow your choice by the use of subtle steering based on racial, religious or other forbidden criteria. Keep in mind, though, that a good agent is a skilled matchmaker, who listens instead of talking and then helps you narrow down available listings for efficient use of your time.
- *Showing of property.* The agent will set up appointments for house inspections and (unless a discount broker) will accompany you. During the tours, don't be afraid to ask questions. The agent will have at hand a wealth of data on each property you see, including lot size, property taxes and assessment figures, age of the house, square footage, heating system and the like.
- *Estimation of ownership costs.* When you are seriously interested in a specific house, your agent will sit down and help you figure out how you could buy it and what it would cost you each month.
- *Contract negotiation.* The agent will prepare either a binding purchase contract or (in some areas) a preliminary memorandum of agreed terms. Differences between what you want and what the seller wants are negotiated until you and the seller reach what is known as a meeting of the minds.
- *Liaison with your attorney, if you use one.* The broker works closely with the attorney from the moment you make your first written offer to purchase.
- *Financing expertise.* This is probably the most important and certainly the most time-consuming of the agent's activities. A skilled agent keeps in close touch with local lending institutions and helps you find the financing that best suits you among hundreds of different mortgage plans.
- *Mortgage application assistance.* In many localities, the agent expects to make an appointment for you with a lending institution, help you prepare for the application interview and perhaps accompany you. While you wait

for loan approval, the agent will keep in touch with the lender to straighten out any hitches that develop.

• *Settlement.* Local customs vary, but in many areas the broker attends the closing session and, in a few places, actually effects the transfer of title.

Chapter 4

*F*iguring Out How Much You Can Spend on Your New Home

*B*ack in the days when pork chops were a nickel apiece and people paid cash for their cars, the rule of thumb was that you could buy a house costing two and one-half times your annual income. The old guideline can still work if interest rates are around 10 percent, you can put 20 percent down and you have few other debts. When rates are as low as 8 percent, you could plan on buying a home costing three times your income.

Otherwise, it's not that simple. Most buyers finance with mortgages these days, and interest rates fluctuate in a way that would have been unthinkable in bygone days. Current thinking concentrates on monthly costs of ownership as they compare with income and debts.

The process of determining how much it's safe for you to borrow is known as *qualifying*. Because a lending institution will qualify you down the line, most good real estate brokers do it, usually with a written interview sheet, when they first meet you. This chapter will help you qualify yourself.

16. Is income the main way they judge eligibility for a loan?

Not really.

Equally important in today's debt-driven society is the amount of your other obligations. Each lending institution and each mortgage plan has its own guidelines. Sometimes you are marked down for any long-standing debt that has more than six months to run, sometimes only for those with a full year or more to go. Outstanding student loans, life insurance payments and child support may affect your allowable mortgage payment, or they may not.

When making your estimate, include all the income of everyone who will own the house. Unmarried persons may pool their income to buy a home together, just as a married couple can. If you are self-employed, average your past two years' income from that source. Do not include one-time events like inheritances, insurance settlements and capital gains.

17. What debts will count against me?

You might not have considered one factor that could weigh against you—the number of credit cards you presently carry. Even if you pay them off promptly and don't carry balances, if you have a whole collection of cards, lenders figure that you could go out tomorrow and borrow up to the hilt on all of them. Particularly if your qualifications are borderline, that possibility might be enough to tip the scales against you. If you have half a dozen cards, consider officially closing most of those accounts as soon as possible, keeping only one or two cards.

Most lenders don't care about debts that will be paid off within six months (in some cases, 10 or 12 months), so when you list your debts, omit those with less than six months to go.

Listing Your Income

	Owner 1	Owner 2
Salary (gross) from primary job		
Self-employment income		
Second job earnings		
Dividends		
Interest		
Pension		
Social Security		
Rental income		
Child support, alimony (if under court order)		
Other		

Total _____ A _____ B

Total income (A + B) = $ _____

18. What are qualifying ratios?

Lenders figure your allowable mortgage payment many different ways. Some calculations even take into account your particular income tax payment and number of dependents. In general, though, you will hear about lending institutions' qualifying ratios. A typical ratio might be 28/36 or (more generous in the amount you could borrow) 29/41.

✏️ Listing Your Monthly Payments

	Owner 1	Owner 2
Car payment		
Furniture loan		
Appliances loan		
Boat or RV loan		
Revolving credit		
Student loan		
Other		
Total	_____ A	_____ B
Total income (A + B) = $	_____	

The first figure is the percentage of your gross monthly income the lender will allow as a maximum monthly payment. With a 28/36 ratio, you would be allowed to spend 28 percent of your monthly gross income on a mortgage payment. This is roughly a week's income for a month's payment because a month contains an average of 4.3 weeks.

Using a 28/36 ratio, a buyer with monthly gross income of $4,000 would be allowed up to $1,120 for a monthly mortgage payment. You can perform the calculation for yourself.

Lenders figure this allowable payment two different ways, however, and the next calculation takes into account your other current debts. The second figure in the ratio we've been using (36 percent) seems to allow a higher percentage of monthly income for mortgage payment, but that's because it must also cover other monthly debt payments.

The same buyer, with monthly gross income of $4,000, might have $400 in present monthly debt payments. Applying the ratio (36 percent) yields $1,440 a month available for debt service. Subtracting present monthly payments of $400 qualifies the borrower for up to $1,040 in mortgage costs.

Lenders figure both ways, then take whichever figure is less, more conservative. (That's why you don't want to go into debt for a new car while you're house hunting.)

✐ Maximum Monthly Payment

Your monthly gross income	$ _____
Multiply by 36%	× _____0.36_____
Maximum monthly debt service	$ _____
Subtract present payments	– _____
Available for monthly payment	$ _____

---

19. What does PITI mean?

The term refers to the four standard components of a monthly mortgage payment: principal, interest, taxes and insurance. With most mortgage plans, the lender will collect each month not only the first two items but also one-twelfth of your yearly property taxes and one-twelfth of your homeowner's insurance premium. Those tax and insurance bills will go directly to the lender, which will pay them with your money, put aside in a separate *escrow* or *trust* account. Lenders are concerned about those particular bills being met, to protect the security for their loans.

How Much for Debt Service?

Your maximum monthly payment (from previous worksheets)	$ _____
Subtract monthly property tax (from agent's estimate)	− _____
Subtract typical insurance	− _____30_____
Principal and interest payment	$ _____

In the example given above, where $1,040 was the maximum PITI payment because the borrower had substantial other debts, how much could this amount buy? For starters, how much mortgage loan could the borrower qualify for?

The answer is not simple.

Property taxes and insurance figures differ from one house to another. Interest rates differ from one mortgage plan to another. And, of course, the amount of cash available for down payment makes a difference. It's relatively simple to make the calculation when you have a particular home already in mind. Nevertheless, you can get a rough estimate.

You'll need information (available from any agent) on average property tax bills in the price range and neighborhood you're aiming for. Homeowner's insurance is a simpler matter because the whole calculation is a rough estimate anyhow; $30 a month might be used. A wrong estimate won't make much difference here.

Assuming that property taxes average $2,400 a year in the neighborhood under consideration, the calculation of mortgage payment would run as follows: $1,040 maximum payment, less $200 a month for taxes, less $30 a month for insurance, which leaves $810 a month for principal and interest. You can run the calculation for yourself, using the lesser of the two final figures from your earlier calculations.

Amortization Schedule: Monthly payment needed to amortize a loan of $1,000				
	Number of Years on the Loan			
	15	**20**	**25**	**30**
Interest Rate (%) 5	7.91	6.60	5.85	5.37
6	8.44	7.17	6.45	6.00
7	8.99	7.76	7.07	6.66
7½	9.28	8.06	7.39	7.00
8	9.56	8.37	7.72	7.34
8½	9.85	8.68	8.05	7.69
9	10.14	9.00	8.39	8.05
9½	10.44	9.33	8.74	8.41
10	10.75	9.66	9.09	8.78
10½	11.05	9.99	9.45	9.15
11	11.37	10.33	9.81	9.53
12	12.00	11.02	10.54	10.29
13	12.65	11.72	11.28	11.07

Then use the amortization table above to estimate how much you might borrow.

If our hypothetical buyer has $30,000 available for a down payment, and he or she can borrow $92,300, the buyer can purchase a home costing about $122,300. For practical purposes, the buyer could look for a property listed for as much as $135,000 because one never knows what a seller will take. The whole calculation is rough anyhow, until exact property taxes and interest rates are known.

✎ How Much Can You Borrow?

Principal and interest payment
(from previous worksheet) $ _____

Divide by monthly cost per
thousand at current rate, 30-year
term (from page 27)   ÷ _____

Number of thousands
multiply by $1,000   × _____1,000_____

Maximum mortgage amount $ _____

✎ How Much for a House?

Maximum mortgage amount (from
previous worksheet) $ _____

Add available down payment   + _____

Estimated purchase price $ _____

The figure is only a rough estimate. You can safely
look at homes priced 10 percent more than that
price.

One caution, now that you've done all this work. Don't be surprised if a skilled agent, working with knowledge of current ratios, interest rates and property taxes, comes up with a different recommendation!

Chapter 5

Really Looking at Homeowning Costs

*Y*our mortgage payment will almost certainly be your largest single expense. It is for most people. If you buy when interest rates are relatively low, you will probably opt for a fixed-rate mortgage. In that case, you can calculate at the start exactly what you'll pay each month for principal and interest for perhaps 15, 25 or 30 years.

When interest rates climb, more borrowers choose adjustable-rate mortgages. If you know the lifetime cap or ceiling on your interest rate, you can calculate the worst case right at the beginning—the highest monthly charge you could ever have if interest rates shoot through the roof sometime during the term of your loan. These mortgage types are discussed in greater detail in Chapter 8.

The next two items in the standard PITI payment are taxes and insurance, which can be handled in one of two ways. You may meet those bills on your own, or—more likely—they will be handled for you by the lending institution.

20. What is an escrow account?

If your home were ever seized and sold for unpaid back taxes, the lending institution would be left with no security for its mortgage; a tax sale wipes out mortgages on the property. If the home burned to the ground, only the vacant lot would remain as security. Or if you're located in a flood plain, your home could conceivably be swept away, with not even the land remaining. So your lender has a direct interest in seeing that you pay your taxes and insurance premiums on time.

With most mortgages, including all VA and FHA loans, an escrow account (reserve, impound, trust account) is set up for you by the lender. Each month, along with your principal and interest payment, you send one-twelfth of your anticipated next property tax and homeowner's insurance (sometimes flood insurance) costs. As the bills come due, they are sent to your lender, which pays them on your behalf.

Your lender is allowed to keep not only enough to pay the next bill due but also a two-month surplus as a precaution. In about half the states, you are entitled to interest on your escrow account.

You will receive regular reports, monthly or at the end of the year, on the status of the escrow account, which is, after all, your own money. At regular intervals, usually yearly, the account will be analyzed and your payment adjusted, up or down, depending on whether the account shows a surplus or deficit.

This adjustment can be a surprise to the homeowner with a fixed-interest mortgage who expected monthly payments to remain exactly the same amount for the full term of the loan. It is, of course, taxes and insurance costs that change, not—with a fixed-interest loan—the underlying principal and interest portion of the payment.

21. Must I keep insurance on the property?

No law requires you to buy insurance, but if you want a mortgage loan, you'll have to. You must prove that you've bought insurance before the lender will turn over the mortgage check to you, and you must name the lender as an interested party on the policy. If you are not required to maintain an escrow account (that's sometimes possible), you can pay the premiums on your own, but the lender is usually entitled to proof, every year, that the bills have been paid.

The mortgagee (lender) will require that you keep what is known as hazard insurance (fire and similar risks) on the property in an amount sufficient to cover the loan. As a prudent homeowner, you will want wider coverage and for a greater amount.

Rebuilding after a fire, even partially, can sometimes cost more than your original purchase price. And you need personal protection for risks that don't concern your lender—liability for a guest who is hurt on your property, for example.

Your best bet is a homeowner's policy, which puts many kinds of insurance together in a package. The least expensive, called basic or HO-1 (homeowner's-1), covers fire, windstorm, explosion, smoke, glass breakage and other perils, including three very important ones: theft, vandalism and liability.

22. What else should I ask when buying insurance?

Besides asking what is covered by the policy you buy, it's important to find out what is *not* covered (earthquakes, floods or pop bottles dropped from airplanes, for example). If you have a valuable collection or expensive jewelry, you may want to pay an additional premium for riders covering those items.

One way to economize on insurance cost is to opt for a larger deductible. This is the portion of your loss you agree to pay yourself. You wouldn't want the bother of filing claims for $150 losses anyway, and you're not buying insurance as a money-making proposition. Agreeing to handle a larger amount of any loss on your own can cut premiums considerably. Insurance is intended to cover real catastrophes, the kind you couldn't handle yourself. Investigate the relative costs at different deductible levels.

23. What's meant by depreciated value?

Suppose your ten-year-old roof is damaged by fire so badly that it must be completely rebuilt. How much is it fair for the insurance company to pay you?

You will end up with a brand-new roof instead of the old one, which was halfway through its useful life. It could be argued that you are entitled to only half the cost of a new roof. On the other hand, you couldn't buy a half-used roof; you would have to spend the money for a completely new one. Through no fault of your own, you would incur an expense you hadn't expected for ten more years.

So it's important to inquire whether the policy will pay full replacement cost, which should be your goal. Sometimes the answer depends on the dollar amount of your coverage; sometimes an inexpensive rider ensures replacement value.

If your home is located in what the federal government considers a flood-prone area according to official maps, you'll have to carry flood insurance before you can get a mortgage loan from a regular lending institution. If flood insurance is difficult to obtain, you can buy it through a federal government program.

This requirement can sometimes be dropped, by the way, if you can submit a survey showing that the lowest part of your building is above the 100-year flood mark.

Even though your condo association carries insurance on your building, you should still carry your own. Though you may feel you own little of value, you might be hard put to replace your stereo set, computer, VCR and TV at the least. Special homeowner's insurance is available for individual condominium units.

If you presently rent, give serious consideration to renter's insurance. Your landlord's policy does not cover your possessions. Renter's insurance is relatively inexpensive.

24. Will my property taxes be the same as the seller's?

In some areas, property taxes remain the same when ownership of a house is transferred, and you can be sure that the tax bill the seller received last year will be the one you receive next year, except for any community-wide increases. In other areas, the assessment (valuation of the house for tax purposes) changes to reflect your purchase price. Next year's taxes would be based on that figure. It's a simple matter to inquire which system is followed in the areas you are considering.

Make sure you know the true tax figure on any house you consider buying. The present owner may have some tax abatement; various possibilities, which differ from one state to another, include senior citizen discounts, veteran tax exemptions and preferential treatment for religious organizations.

On the other hand, the seller's tax figure may be more than the true tax figure. In some localities, for example, unpaid water bills are added to the tax bill. On rare occasions, a seller who neglects property could have costs for grass cutting and even repairs by the city added to the tax bill.

Find out whether taxes in your state are paid in advance, for the coming fiscal year, or in arrears, at the end of the tax year. If you consider buying a brand-new house, remember that present taxes are probably based on the value of the vacant lot; the exact amount you will be paying may or may not be established at the time you buy. You can always inquire of the local tax department approximately how much that would be.

25. What other costs should I look into?

Find out whether trash collection is included in taxes and whether there is any extra charge for services like sidewalk snowplowing. Inquire about sewer and water charges. Ask the sellers about their utility and fuel bills for the past year or, better yet, for two years back.

Include in your calculation of monthly costs the price of basic telephone service and, for most households, cable TV; those figures may vary from one locality to another. Compare costs on homes you consider purchasing.

26. What's the difference between repairs and improvements, and why does it matter?

Improvements are just that—permanent additions that increase the value of your home. Every homeowner should keep a permanent file detailing all expenses for improvements, including bills, checks and receipts. The Internal Revenue Service considers your cost basis for the home to include not only original purchase price but also money spent on improvements.

Repairs and redecorating are not considered improvements. Patching the roof is a repair; installing a complete new one counts as an improvement. Repainting your living room doesn't count; painting a new wing does. Other improvements include putting in a fence; paving the driveway, installing a new furnace, new wiring or wall-to-wall carpeting; finishing the basement; and adding new rooms. Even a few dollars spent on a new towel rack can be added to your cost basis.

27. How much is safe to put into improving my new home?

Few improvements increase the resale value of your property by the amount you spend on them. Buyers may like the idea of a finished basement but seldom want to pay anything extra for it. Depending on the location of the property and neighborhood price levels and expectations, an in-ground swimming pool may add value or may actually be a detriment when the time comes to sell. Make improvements for your own satisfaction, not necessarily as investments.

It is financially unwise to overimprove a house beyond its neighbors. When you sell such a home, it's almost impossible to recoup your investment. A given street will support only a given price range; after that, buyers with more to spend want to live on a more prestigious street. As you house hunt, keep in mind that any planning for alterations and additions is risky if it will make yours the most expensive house on the street.

On the other hand, you may pick up a bargain from owners who have put too much money into their home and can't get it out.

Chapter 6

*C*hoosing the Perfect Home for You

*R*emember to look ahead when you envision your dream home. You may be sure about what you want now, but think about the future as you begin your search. Unless you are willing to move every few years, try to anticipate some of the changes that lie in your future.

Nature-loving newlyweds may come into an agent's office asking for "an old house—we don't care if it's run down because we can work on it, but it has to be in the country on five acres." (There's something magic about five acres; no one ever requests four acres or six and a half.)

The agent faces a problem immediately because it can be difficult to find financing for a run-down house. And a few years later, the couple may come back to the office, having found themselves isolated with two toddlers and nary a babysitter in sight.

"Please," they say, "this time show us something in the middle of a tract full of playmates and teenage girls."

Ideas about housing design can change also. Our couple with the little ones might be delighted with a family room open to the kitchen so that the tots can be supervised while the cooking is going on. But ten years later, the parents might long for a family room located down a flight of stairs, around a corner and with a soundproof door.

Every home is a compromise. Before you start looking, accept the fact that you will eventually give up something you now consider important: the mature trees, the open fireplace, the guest room. You'll fall in love with one special home and suddenly decide you can live without a sunny backyard after all.

28. What should I know about floor plans?

Keep in mind a few basics as you inspect houses. Stand in the entrance, and try to imagine yourself going about the daily routine. Consider, for example, a hypothetical trip home with bags of groceries. Where will you park? Will you have to carry the load up stairs? Must you go through the living room to get to the kitchen? Is there a handy counter near the refrigerator for unloading?

If you have an infant, you might sleep with your door open and want to be within earshot of the baby's room. In a year or two, though, you will value a private, quiet bedroom. Check whether the master bedroom is separated from the others by a zone of closets, hallway or baths. (The best floor plans incorporate such buffers for all bedrooms.)

If the front door opens directly into the living room, a house in the North will need a small enclosed foyer to shield the thermostat from icy blasts. Then imagine yourself in midsummer, eating on the enclosed porch or patio. Will it be easy to serve from the kitchen, without risking spills on the living room carpet en route?

Check the kitchen for sufficient counter and cupboard space. Double-check for a place to put things down, not only next to the refrigerator but also near the stove and sink. Even if you are resigned to a small "Pullman" kitchen and plan to eat in the dining room, look for enough space for a high chair or a stool for a chatty guest.

Give a house extra points if you don't have to go through the living room to reach other areas. A dead-end living room makes for relaxation and tends to stay neat. Look for the convenience of an outside entrance to the basement and an outside door to the garage.

An engineer's inspection can help you evaluate condition and is particularly valuable with an older home, but you are the only one who can judge whether a floor plan fits your lifestyle.

29. If I buy a brand-new house, what should I watch out for?

Buying a house that's newly built, you need to be concerned about a warranty for faults that may show up during the first year. The possibilities of negotiating on price with a builder or developer are limited; price is based on cost and, except in hardship situations, usually is not too flexible. It may be possible, though, to dicker for extras that otherwise involve add-on prices.

In many areas, you may not know what property taxes will be levied on new construction; a talk with the assessor's office is in order.

It's important to get all promises in writing. If possible, have your attorney arrange for part of the purchase price to be held in escrow, pending the builder's attention to small matters that may come up during your first few months' occupancy.

Having a house custom-built to one's own specifications is a favorite daydream for many people. The chance to pick the right lot, site the house as you want and create an environment that reflects your taste and personality is seductive.

30. What are the drawbacks to building my own home?

Before you enter such an undertaking, be aware that everything will take longer than expected; everything will cost more than expected; the weather will turn uncooperative; changing your mind about anything as you go along will be amazingly expensive; your marriage will be strained by constant decisions and different points of view; and large amounts of your own time and attention will be required, even if you work with the best contractor foreman.

To protect yourself, check your builder's or contractor's record with your state's attorney general's office or whatever state agency supervises such work. Contact recent customers to see how satisfied they are.

Make sure your contractor carries proper insurance. Don't allow any avoidance of required building permits and inspections. Insist on proof that subcontractors and suppliers are being paid by the general contractor, and never hand over final installments until you're sure the work is completely satisfactory.

31. Are there advantages to owning an apartment?

In areas where land is at a premium, cooperatives and condominium apartments may be attractive alternatives to more expensive housing. Many empty-nesters and busy young professionals also enjoy the absence of outside chores. It's easy to just lock the door and travel without worrying. Such apartments combine the advantages of homeowning with the convenience of apartment living. The IRS treats co-ops and condos exactly as it does single-family houses.

The *cooperative* is the older form of ownership, found mainly in New York City, Chicago and a few other areas. The owner of a co-op does not own any real estate. Rather, the buyer receives two things: shares in a corporation that owns the entire building and a proprietary lease for the particular living unit being bought.

These shares and the lease are classified not as real estate but as personal property. They may be borrowed against, however, to assist with the purchase, and the IRS will treat the loan as if it were a mortgage. The owner of a co-op does not owe any property tax on the individual living unit. Instead, the monthly payment includes a share of taxes paid by the cooperative on the entire building. It also includes a share of the cooperative's payment on the one large mortgage on the entire building, as well as the usual maintenance costs.

Tenant-owners in a cooperative building depend on each other for financial stability. For that reason, most co-ops require that prospective buyers be approved by the board of directors.

Because a large part of the monthly charge goes toward property taxes and interest on the underlying mortgage, the prospective buyer can expect a certain percentage of that expenditure to be income tax deductible at the end of the year. If you are interested in a cooperative, you will be told what percentage of the monthly charge is deductible. Inquire also about the dollar amount of liability you will be taking on for your share of the existing mortgage on the whole building. This will be in addition to any loan you place to buy your shares.

The term *condominium* describes a form of ownership rather than—as is usually assumed—an apartment. The buyer of a condominium receives a deed and owns real estate, just as a single house would be owned. In the case of a condominium, the buyer receives complete title to the interior of the apartment ("from the plaster in") and also to a percentage of the common elements—the land itself, staircases, sidewalks, swimming pool, driveways, lawns, elevators, roofs, heating systems.

The condominium is classified as real estate, and the buyer may place a mortgage on the property and will receive an individual tax bill for the one unit. In addition, monthly fees are levied to pay for outside maintenance, repairs, landscaping, snow removal, recreation facilities and the like.

32. What should I watch out for when buying a condo?

Be sure to ask about parking: How far from your unit will it be? Are you entitled to more than one space? Where will your guests park?

Before buying any type of apartment, you should receive a daunting amount of material to read. Look it over carefully. Enlist the aid of an accountant and/or attorney to review the material. Pay particular attention to five things:

1. The financial health of the organization you will join; does it have substantial reserves to cover major renovations and replacements?
2. The condition of the building(s); is it likely to need a new roof or boiler or replacement windows or elevators, for which you would bear a share of responsibility?
3. The covenants, conditions and regulations you must promise to observe; could you rent out your apartment, install awnings, paint your front door red, plant tomatoes anywhere or eventually sell the unit on the open market?
4. Any special assessments that are expected in the near future. It helps if you can get a written answer to this one, or at least something said in front of witnesses. If all the skylights have been leaking recently, or chimneys need repointing, you might find yourself hit with an unexpected bill soon after you move in.
5. The percentage of owner-occupancy. Traditionally, more homeowners and fewer tenants is the preferred situation.

33. What's different about a town house?

Architecturally, a town house is an attached, usually up-and-down house of the sort known in some cities as a row house.

Town house ownership is a hybrid type of condominium and/or cooperative and can take many forms. Typically, the unit owner has fee simple (complete) ownership of the living space and the land below it, with some form of group ownership of common areas. The individual may or may not own a small patio or front area and may or may not own the roof above the unit. As with an old-fashioned row house, there is usually no other unit above the town house.

Common areas are owned by a homeowners' association, and several forms of legal organization are possible.

34. Is a mobile home a good investment?

The answer depends, in large part, on where you live in this country.

In many areas, particularly in the South and West, mobile homes are a way of life for a large proportion of the population. One attraction is the lower initial cost, as compared with a completely furnished single-family home. One problem is finding the lot on which you can put your mobile home; some communities are zoned against them.

Many mobile homes, therefore, are placed on rented land. In this case, they are classified as personal property rather than real estate. If the home sits on a foundation and on its own land, however, it does count as real estate.

Out in the country, the mobile home is likely to use a septic system. Be sure to ask some specific questions about the system's capacity and overall condition.

Choosing the mobile-home community into which you buy may be more important than picking the individual home itself. Talk with occupants of the development; find out how cooperative and well staffed the management is. Although the home is yours, to some extent you will be a tenant—and a fairly captive one because mobile homes are not very mobile and you are not likely to move yours to another location.

Give some consideration to buying a used mobile home. Brand-new ones in some areas depreciate in value like brand-new automobiles. You may pick up a bargain in a used one and stand a better chance of recouping your investment or even—in a choice development—seeing some profit when you sell in the future.

The right mobile home can be a pleasant and relatively inexpensive way of living, but it will almost never appreciate in value as a site-built house would. Used mobile homes compete with brand-new ones full of brand-new furniture and appliances when it's time to resell, and that sets a limit on their value.

Chapter 7

*F*inding Great Homebuying Bargains

*W*hen a young couple walks into a REALTOR®'s office carrying a clipboard, the agent suspects one of them is an engineer. It seems to go with the training. Taking notes would be a good way for you to approach your house hunting, too. Another good way to look at real estate is without children so you can concentrate on the job at hand.

Inspecting houses is a tiring and confusing process. If you look at more than four in a morning or an afternoon, you'll end up with your head in a whirl. Lying in bed that night, you'll try in vain to remember whether it was the brick ranch or the Victorian that backed up to the expressway. You'll be totally unable to recall which place boasted the purple kitchen. It can be helpful to take along a Polaroid or video camera to record such things (often an agent has one or can borrow one from the office).

Ask the agent for data on each property, and take that information home with you. In order to concentrate fully on the real estate, wait to make your notes until you have finished looking, possibly when you are back in the car. Jot down your impressions on the computer printouts or copies of the listing sheets for the homes you inspect.

If you note the things you dislike about a place or which features really appeal to you, sorting it out later becomes easier. You may want to mark up a street map of the area, locating the houses you view and also noting schools, religious institutions, shopping areas and other amenities.

35. I think I may move within a few years after I buy. Are there special points to keep in mind?

If you may need to sell your new home before long, buy carefully. Avoid anything unique, which might require a long search before you found someone else who shares your taste. Buy as inexpensive a house as you can feel comfortable in so that you can tap into the largest possible pool of prospective buyers.

The ideal resale house is probably a fairly modern three-bedroom tract house in an area full of young families and with a good school system.

36. Are there really any bargains out there?

There are indeed, and after you've been looking a while, you'll be able to spot them.

As you park across the street from the house on Robin Circle, your agent says apologetically, "Now, I want to warn you, there are a lot of kids in this house, school's out, and it doesn't show too well." Without moving from the car, you can see an old pickup truck in the driveway, a shaggy lawn, rusted toys on the front walk, old flyers mouldering under the shrubs and a torn screen door.

A disaster?

No, an opportunity.

When you locate such a home, if it has had decent mainte-nance (as opposed to housekeeping), you have stumbled upon a bargain. Houses that have been rented out sometimes fall into this category.

Most buyers cannot see past sloppiness. Perhaps without even knowing why, they say that "the place doesn't have good vibes." As a result, the house on Robin Circle—and many homes like it—may stay on the market for months and may eventually sell for as much as 10 percent less than true market value.

On the other hand, as you walk into a spotless house, try to ignore the smell of gingerbread wafting through the place, your own favorite music playing softly and the flowers on the design-er coffee table. Of course, such a home has probably had fine care, and it could be a pleasure to move into. Still, when the sellers move out, they will take the gingerbread pan, the coffee table, the CD player and those great speakers. You will be left with just three things: the location, the floor plan and the condition.

If those factors—apart from surface appeal—seem right to you, don't hesitate to put in your offer for such a home. It will sell quickly. If it also has been underpriced, emergency action is indicated, as described in Chapter 9. More commonly, a house that shows well commands a premium.

When it comes to decorating and housekeeping, try to ignore the sizzle; concentrate on the steak. Pay attention to location, layout and basic condition. Location can't be changed, floor plan can be altered only at some expense, but the last factor—condition—can be remedied. Just be sure, if there's a problem, that you know what you're getting into. An engineering report can tell you exactly what to expect.

Bargains also can be found where sellers are under pressure. The seller's broker won't—or shouldn't, at any rate—reveal that the home is near foreclosure or the seller is going bankrupt. But you can see for yourself sometimes—if it's a divorce situation, if the home is vacant or doesn't look lived in, if she's on the new job in Chicago and he's here alone with three kids and big long-distance phone bills. Such sellers may be ready to deal and ready to trade a price concession for a quick sale.

Where the owner has died, an executor is sometimes amenable to any reasonable offer in return for a prompt, trouble-free winding up of the estate. An older person suspicious of workmen and short on cash may not want to bring a long-owned home up to standards required by a lending institution; sometimes a broker can help you work out a mutually beneficial arrangement to solve that impasse.

Above all, the way to buy a bargain is to buy promptly. The buying public is a sensitive judge of value. A house that is mistakenly underpriced will be snapped up quickly. For that reason, it's sensible to invest some time in learning the market and helpful to locate a broker in whose advice you have confidence.

37. What are the most important factors in value?

Before you are very far into your house hunting, someone will tell you the oldest real estate joke (almost the only real estate joke): the three most important factors in the value of a house are (1) location, (2) location and (3) location.

It's true, too. A house costing $600,000 in Beverly Hills might sell, on a comparable lot in the suburbs of Peoria, for $100,000. Never in the history of this country have locational differences been so marked. Closer to home, you know yourself that a modest house in the most expensive suburb is worth much more than an almost identical property in an inner-city neighborhood.

From a buyer's point of view, you have two ways of looking at this locational preference, which appraisers call *situs*. The classic advice is to buy the modest house on a more expensive street. Such a property is easy to resell, and its value will hold up well because there are always buyers eager for the prestige of that particular neighborhood. And remodeling or adding to it is possible because alterations won't push it out of the price range for that area.

On the other hand, the most luxurious house on the street won't ever repay the owner for the money invested. No matter how elegant it may be, buyers with money to spend will aim at another, fancier neighborhood.

In one way, then, an overimproved house represents an opportunity for the buyer who wants lots of space and luxury features and isn't worried about resale value. If you think you will live in the house for a long time, and if you like the area, you may be able to pick up a great deal for your money.

$38.$ Are there really bargains in foreclosed properties?

Forget the TV gurus who promise you can pick up a house for a dollar. But yes, there are bargains to be had in foreclosures. What they don't tell you are the drawbacks. It's not a process to be undertaken lightly.

Foreclosed property is sold at public auction (in some locations, described as "on the courthouse steps," which it actually is). If you attend an auction, you may be surprised to find the mortgage lender starting the bidding at the amount owed; the good part is that sometimes one dollar above that will take it.

One drawback is that you must buy for cash, or nearly so. You must furnish immediately a certified check for perhaps 10 percent, and you might be offered something like a month to come up with the rest of the money. That may or may not be enough time to arrange a mortgage loan—and you or the property might not meet the lender's standards for a loan in time.

Another problem is that the unfortunate owner need not let you in to inspect the property before you bid on it; you'll have to take your chances sight unseen. And many times, an owner who can't pay the mortgage hasn't kept up with repairs either; the place may need some work.

If you want to try for foreclosures, you'll find them advertised in at least one local newspaper. You can contact the law firm mentioned in the ad for details. It's best to have your own lawyer guide you through the procedure, which varies from one locality to another.

Foreclosed property offered by HUD (FHA) or VA is a bit different. The houses are already owned by the government and are vacant, some of them renovated. Mortgages are available if you qualify. The properties are usually described in local newspaper ads, with addresses, number of rooms and minimum bids listed. You can inspect the houses by contacting local brokers, who will have keys to open them. To make an offer, you work through regular real estate agencies, which forward the paperwork to the agency involved, along with your earnest money deposit. Sealed bids are opened at the same time, and you will hear fairly promptly whether you are successful.

A house you buy in that fashion may well go for less than market value, but it won't be dirt-cheap, as they promise on those get-rich-quick television programs.

To sum up, then, you can sometimes find bargains in:

- Sloppy houses, otherwise well maintained
- Real estate owned by families in stress: divorce, death, illness
- Property overimproved for its neighborhood
- Foreclosed property

39. How can I choose a neighborhood?

If you are moving just across town, you probably know what area suits your lifestyle best. Coming to a new community, however, requires research. Real estate brokers must, by the nature of their work, help you narrow your options if you are ever to settle on one house. Rigorously regulated by human rights law, however, brokers hesitate to characterize neighborhoods or give opinions on school systems. If their assumptions are based on the forbidden factors—race, color, religion, country of origin, age, disability, sex—they could face charges of illegal *steering* (using subtle means to ensure that you end up where they think you should).

Brokers can, however, furnish solid data, and a good agent will have information available: per-pupil expenditure in various school systems, number of graduates going on to four-year colleges and the like.

One good way to learn about a new community is to subscribe to its local newspaper. Read it carefully for a few weeks, and you'll begin to get a feeling for neighborhoods. In the end, you will have to decide yourself which areas you want to consider.

40. What if nothing comes on the market in the area I like?

If you really want to live there, you might try leafletting the neighborhood. One young lawyer wrote a one-page letter describing his family, explaining that he particularly wanted to live in a certain neighborhood and asking whether anyone was interested in selling. He stressed that he was not a real estate broker looking for listings. By the time he returned home from distributing the leaflets, two homeowners had left messages on his answering machine—and he bought one of the homes.

41. What should I watch for in an older house?

If you want to buy an older house, you will probably use the services of a home inspector but you won't want that expense for every house you consider. Therefore, it's worth doing a little preinspecting yourself.

In general, houses built since World War II are more or less modern. In these, you can pretty much count on copper plumbing, adequate electric service and a furnace that is at least compact. Houses more than 20 years old, however, require extra-careful inspection. You won't look in detail at every house you see, but when you seriously consider making an offer on one, go over it carefully.

Start with the outside of the house. Does it have easy-care features—built-in sprinklers in a dry climate or self-storing storm windows up north? How soon might the place need a coat of paint?

Examine the roof; binoculars can be of help here. Look for missing or curled shingles, patched spots or a dried-up, crinkled appearance. Moss growing on the roof indicates a moisture problem. And if in midwinter every other roof on the street bears a load of snow while this one is clean, you are looking at a house with inadequate insulation.

In termite areas (the Southeast and Southwest), look for mud tubes where wooden parts of the porch or foundation adjoin the ground. Poke exposed wood to see whether it is solid.

In some northern areas, termites are just about unheard of, but you might run into carpenter ants. Look for small piles of fine sawdust below ceiling beams. Prod floor joists, if they are exposed in the cellar, to check for soft spots.

Downspouts should be firmly attached. Gutters lose points if little trees grow out of them. If they need only repainting, that's a minor matter, but gutters with holes in them will need replacing.

The homeowner's warranty a seller may furnish looks reassuring, and it can't do any harm. Don't choose your home just because a warranty is offered, however. Those policies usually do not cover structural defects, and they may have high deductibles you'd have to pay on your own if a repair were needed.

42. What do I need in electric service?

Remember that many homes built around the turn of the century didn't originally have any electric service. If the initial installation hasn't been updated, it can be inadequate for anything beyond the light bulbs, refrigerator and flatiron it was designed for. The proliferation of appliances these days calls for plenty of outlets. You want 100-amp service at a minimum, 220 amps for electric stoves and some clothes dryers and air conditioners. Look for an outlet every 12 feet on a long wall so that any six-foot cord can be plugged in without an extension cord. Small rooms should have at least one outlet on each wall.

Upstairs, be alert for any tangle of extension cords, which can indicate inadequate outlets. Downstairs, examine the fuse box. If you find circuit breakers, you will know that the service has been modernized. But there is nothing wrong with an old-fashioned fuse system if it is extensive enough for your needs and was carefully installed.

43. What matters as far as plumbing is concerned?

More expensive to remedy than inadequate wiring is faulty plumbing. You hope to find all the old galvanized pipes replaced with copper. Galvanized pipe suffers from corrosion and eventually develops hardening of the arteries, with deposits narrowing the inside until flow is impeded. This happens first with the horizontal hot-water lines, so check by starting outward from the water heater.

What you don't want to see is a patch job, where a single emergency was solved by putting a length of copper pipe into old galvanized tubing. Such a joint signals a serious chemical reaction ahead. Eventually, someone will have to rip out the whole line and replace it with copper, and that someone might be you.

If the house has modernized kitchen and baths, it's likely that the whole plumbing system was updated when they were installed. If you're in doubt, ask.

If the home has a well, you'll want proof of water quality and flow. If a septic system is used, ask questions about legal installation and past performance. (If sewers are available but not connected, you may have trouble securing a mortgage loan.)

44. Should I hold out for a completely dry basement?

In some areas, buyers are understandably worried about a basement that might develop a running stream during spring thaws or summer storms. One quick way to judge is to see how much junk an owner stores directly on the basement floor. Piles of very old newspapers may mean a packrat mentality—and a dry basement.

To determine whether a basement has flooded, inspect the bottom of the furnace and the water heater. Rust, or a newly painted neat strip across the bottom few inches, calls for an explanation. If a one-time flood (which can happen in the best of homes) occurred while the furnace was hot, the firebox may be cracked.

Small amounts of dampness on basement walls, though, are almost standard in some localities.

If an older house in a cold climate hasn't been adequately insulated, you should do it yourself immediately. The best place for insulation is under the attic floor. Look for holes in the stair risers that were drilled for blown-in insulation and then plugged. Try to find out how many inches were installed. Some old jobs were very good indeed; others don't meet modern standards.

Another simple installation with a fine payback is band insulation around the top of the basement wall, where the foundation meets the floor joists.

If the house lacks insulation or storm windows, inquire, when it comes time to apply for a mortgage, about whether you may include the cost of energy-savers in your mortgage.

Don't pay a big premium just because the house has sidewall insulation. It's nice, of course, but it doesn't have the payback of that thick layer under the attic floor.

45. What environmental hazards might I run into?

High-Voltage Lines.   Scientists still debate the effect of electromagnetic radiation, particularly on children. Some early studies indicate increased rates of cancer in those who live close to high-voltage lines. There's not yet a dependable guideline in this matter; emissions are easily tested, however.

Radon.   One toxic substance you can't see for yourself is radon, a colorless, odorless, gas that seeps into houses from the earth itself. The Environmental Protection Agency (EPA) considers radon second only to cigarette smoke as a cause of lung cancer. "It's like exposing your family to hundreds of chest X-rays a year," says the EPA. The agency estimates that one house in five has unacceptable levels of radon. Testing can be unreliable unless carefully done, best by a professional. Simply using a test kit can yield false results if windows are kept open during the test, which takes several days. Some areas are at higher risk than others. Fortunately, curing a radon problem is relatively simple and inexpensive, usually requiring specific ventilation in the foundation and basement.

Lead.   High levels of lead in children have been shown to affect mental and physical development. Lead paint is no longer used, but for most loans anyone considering a house built before 1978 must receive a written information sheet discussing it. Chipping paint is particularly dangerous. As with asbestos, removing lead paint can release dangerous amounts of the substance; sometimes the best solution is to cover it. If the paint is to be removed, safety precautions must be taken.

Asbestos.   This fireproof mineral was widely used before about 1975 in all sorts of building materials, from insulation to floor tiles. Its tiny fibers can cause lung cancer. Where it is intact and not deteriorating, asbestos poses little or no danger. The most common problem may be heavy insulation wrapped around heat ducts from an old-fashioned furnace. Removing the insulation releases the fibers; sometimes a problem is best solved by encasing the material.

46. Do I need a professional inspection?

First-time homebuyers often call in parents, uncles or best friends for advice on a home they're considering. Unfortunately, the amateur expert usually feels duty-bound to find something wrong with the property, and the buyer ends up even more confused. It's best to get your estimate of condition from a professional. You may be charged a few hundred dollars for the inspection, depending on travel time, but it could be well worth it.

In many communities, home inspection services provided by licensed engineers are available. (See the yellow pages under "Building Inspectors" or "Home Inspectors.") Those who belong to the American Society of Home Inspectors (ASHI) have met specific standards of education and experience. Ask whether a particular inspector does repair work or recommends contractors; if the answer is yes, look for another inspector. You want someone who has nothing to gain by finding fault with the property.

You can hire an inspector before or after you make an offer on a home; Chapter 9 has information on how to make your purchase offer dependent upon a satisfactory report.

Try to accompany your inspector with a tape recorder. You'll learn many interesting things about the house that would not be in the written report. The engineer can't tell you what the house is worth or give you advice on whether to buy it. Instead, you'll hear things like "That roof looks as if it has another five years or so on it. If you had to replace it today, it might cost. . . ." Making the final decision is up to you.

Ask specifically whether there are indications that the house needs a specialist's inspection for a toxic substance.

47. Is it a good idea to visit open houses?

It's a fine way to start. Usually held on Saturday or Sunday afternoons, they are invitations to the general public. You won't need any advance appointment or research; you can tour the neighborhoods that most interest you, stopping in at one house after another. It's a great way to get a feeling for prices.

Don't hesitate to visit even if you're not ready to buy. Brokers can be lonely, giving up a Sunday afternoon to sit in a house, and will welcome you. Don't be worried if you're asked to sign in. If it were your home, wouldn't you want people to identify themselves before they came in? And, of course, you'll wipe your feet, restrain your children and put out your cigarette before entering.

Community practices differ in the matter of open-house etiquette among brokers. If you work with one agent, discuss frankly the best way to visit open houses on your own when he or she isn't available. You don't want to find your dream home, only to find that you've stepped into jurisdictional disputes. Most agents can offer suggestions on how to head off such problems.

48. What if I find a house my broker hasn't suggested?

Of course, you'll read the ads avidly while you house hunt. Particular real estate terms common to each area may puzzle you; don't hesitate to ask your agent to explain them.

If you want to work through your own buyer's broker, or the one seller's agent who gives you good service, don't answer ads yourself. Phone the agent, and mention the items that catch your eye.

The broker can then do a little investigating, particularly where the Multiple Listing Service is involved. Then you'll receive a call back: "That ad on page five was the house I showed you last week; it sure looks different on paper, doesn't it? The one on the bottom of the page is about $60,000 more than your price range. But the one on page six was just listed yesterday, and it sounds as if you might like it. I arranged with the listing agent for us to view it this afternoon."

Chapter 8

*U*nderstanding All of Your Financing Options

*A*sking "What is the best type of mortgage?" is like walking into a pharmacy and asking "What's your best medicine?" The answer, of course, depends on what sort of ailment you're trying to treat.

More than a hundred mortgage plans are probably available right now in your area, and each one fits the needs of a particular buyer, seller or parcel of real estate.

If you're like most buyers, the first place to go for guidance is an agent, either your own or a seller's. Within the first few minutes of conversation, a good agent begins, almost unconsciously, to plan a strategy for financing your loan. Those impertinent questions about your salary, cash on hand and present debts are important in helping you find the right way to manage your purchase.

Mortgage brokers, who bring borrowers and lenders together, also can be helpful. In most cases, they are paid by lenders, or by buyers only after a loan is secured.

49. I can buy for all cash; is that a good idea?

Like all financial planning questions, this one really requires the answer "It all depends"—on your age, income, assets and the like. But simply as a homebuying strategy, a purchase for all cash is, of course, the simplest and quickest method. It is also the most welcome to a seller and, in a normal open market sale, should be worth a concession on price.

You may run into an unusual situation that calls for immediate action—a seller facing foreclosure, for example. Sometimes, when a divorce or death occurs in a family, an owner will accept a bargain price in return for quick cash.

If you do buy for all cash, you need to be extra careful. In an "act right now" situation, resist the temptation to negotiate without legal advice. You may need to sign an immediate purchase offer promising prompt settlement, but your own lawyer should ensure that the offer protects you properly.

Without the protection of a mortgage lender's investigation, you need assurance that you are receiving clear, trouble-free title, that taxes are paid to date, that the seller has the right to transfer the property to you and that you aren't taking over old financial claims along with the real estate.

50. Is it really possible to buy with no money down?

You've seen those hot-shot speakers on cable TV. Can you really buy real estate with nothing down?

Yes, indeed.

There are several ways. And they're no secret. You don't need to send $299 for the books and tapes, even if operators are standing by to take your call. Any good real estate broker knows the techniques and can tell you whether a particular plan fits your circumstances.

Veterans can place VA loans with nothing down—and do it on houses valued at more than $200,000—if they qualify to carry the payments. If a seller agrees, a VA loan can even be placed with the seller furnishing all the buyer's closing costs.

Particularly with income property, where the owner doesn't need to get the money out right away, you can always look for a seller who will turn over the property to you, finance your purchase and take back a mortgage, perhaps requiring nothing down (if you look really good).

And although they're not available with no money down, many conventional mortgage plans require a minimum of only 5 percent, with Federal Housing Administration (FHA) loans asking a bit less.

For the usual home purchase, a smorgasbord of mortgage types is spread out for your consideration. Dozens of terms describe particular mortgages: FHA, VA, assumable, purchase-money, second, package, balloon, portfolio, conventional, convertible, adjustable-rate, fixed-rate. An agent contemplates this dazzling array, trying to fit your needs with current offerings (lenders call them product—"We have some great new product this week" means "We've come up with yet another financing twist").

Picking the right loan involves taking into consideration many factors beyond the quoted rate of interest. These include proposed down payment, your income and future prospects and plans, the seller's finances, current trends in interest rates, type and condition of the property, and costs and fees.

When you're offered a loan at a particularly favorable rate, inquire about closing costs. Certain costs are standard: points, appraisal of the property, a credit check on yourself and other legitimate charges. But some lenders inflate their profit with fake junk fees or garbage fees, which might be listed as underwriting fees, document processing charges, commitment fees and the like.

In some states, including California, a slightly different legal system uses a deed of trust instead of a mortgage. If your state is one of these, for practical purposes you can consider *deed of trust* and *mortgage* to be interchangeable terms.

51. What is meant by a portfolio loan?

In looking for the right mortgage plan, it helps to understand the difference between portfolio loans and those intended for the secondary market.

Years ago, banks took part of their depositors' savings, lent it out on mortgages, collected monthly payments and, when enough money was returned, made more loans. This procedure is the exception these days. The bank that uses such a system is said to make portfolio or nonconforming loans, keeping the mortgages as assets in its own portfolio.

Most other mortgages, these days, are bundled into large packages and sold to big investors in what is known as the secondary market. Among the buyers are large insurance companies, banks, pension funds and, most important, organizations specifically set up to warehouse mortgages, like the Federal National Mortgage Association (Fannie Mae).

You will probably not be notified if your mortgage is sold. You may not realize it if the original lender retains the servicing—collecting payments, handling paperwork and forwarding the money. In other cases, particularly when the buyer of the packaged mortgages is another bank, borrowers may be instructed to send their payments directly to the new mortgagee. Many borrowers feel betrayed when they find they must deal with out-of-state institutions instead of their friendly local banks, but the system allows lenders to recoup their investment immediately and to channel more mortgage money back into the community.

Lenders are required to notify you, before commitment, how likely your loan is to be sold on the secondary market. And if the servicing is transferred, you are entitled to ample advance notice.

All of this can affect your search for the perfect mortgage. When most lenders have identical top limits on the amount they'll lend, or analyze your income in the same way, they probably plan to package your loan and sell it, and are conforming to the requirements of the secondary market.

If you have an unusual situation—complicated self-employment income, the desire to pay your own property taxes and insurance rather than use the lender's escrow account or a 200-year-old house that doesn't meet today's standards, for example—find out which local lenders are currently making portfolio loans. With these loans, they can be more flexible, making exceptions to their usual rules, subject only to state laws and their own judgment. Portfolio loans are sometimes said to be nonconforming because they are not tailored to the requirements of the secondary market, or jumbo loans if they are for larger amounts than the secondary market will buy.

The term *underwriting* refers to the process of analyzing a mortgage application, looking over the paperwork exhibits (appraisal or inspection of the property, verification of employment, credit report, etc.) and making a decision about furnishing the loan. Underwriters decide which loans look safe and can be forwarded to their mortgage committees for approval.

52. Where do I go to get a mortgage?

Hold on! Remember—you're going to *give* the lender a mortgage, a claim on your property, in return for a loan. What you're looking for is a lender that will take your mortgage, hold your mortgage. You are trying to place your mortgage. You're looking for a mortgage *loan.*

Don't be surprised if your lender turns out to be something different from the traditional "bank"—savings bank, commercial bank or savings and loan institution. While those entities are still very much in the mortgage business, new players have emerged.

Mortgage bankers (mortgage companies) are in business solely to make (originate) mortgage loans and handle the ensuing monthly paperwork (servicing). Unlike traditional banks, they take no depositors' savings, offer no checking accounts. They are active in the secondary market, selling packages of mortgages and turning the proceeds back into the community to make more loans. Mortgage banking firms have become a large part of the lending scene in the past decade.

Credit unions are often overlooked in the search for the right lender. If you belong to one, mention this fact to the broker with whom you are working and investigate for yourself whether your credit union offers mortgage loans. In some instances, favorable terms are available.

Mortgage brokers make no loans at all. Their role is to bring borrowers and lenders together. If you have an unusual situation or special needs, they can be particularly useful because they may keep current with the offerings of many different lenders. Think twice, though, about paying a commission up front, before you secure a loan commitment. Not all mortgage brokers require a prepaid commission.

53. What are points, and will I have to pay them?

As with everything else, there are good points and bad points. Bad points are the ones you pay; good points are the ones someone else pays. They are charged by lending institutions as extra up-front, one-time, lump-sum interest when a new loan is placed.

Each point is 1 percent of a new loan. If you buy a home for $150,000 and borrow $120,000, for example, one point would equal $1,200 (not $1,500). Two points would be $2,400. The term is sometimes used interchangeably with *percent,* as in "You'll have a two-point cap," which means you'd have a 2 percent cap.

Points are usually paid at final settlement, when the loan is actually made, or—occasionally—at the time of mortgage application (in which case, find out whether they are refundable if the loan does not go through).

Sometimes you can pay extra points in return for special favors—for example, a lock-in that guarantees you'll receive the interest rate in effect when you apply for the loan, no matter what happens to rates in the meantime (but what if rates go down before your closing?). Or you may be charged extra for an extension if you don't close within a given period after the bank commits to making the loan.

During negotiation of a sales contract, the seller will sometimes agree to pay the buyer's points, simply to expedite the sale. This can be particularly useful if the buyer is short on cash for closing.

Points paid by you as the buyer of your own residence are income tax deductible as interest, in the year they are paid. Points you pay to purchase income property must be amortized (deducted bit by bit over the years), along with other costs of placing an investor's loan.

Points paid by the seller are one of the expenses of selling, and they reduce the seller's capital gain on the sale. The buyer, however, is allowed to take points paid by either party as an income tax deduction for interest expense for that year. Talk about double-dipping on the IRS!

54. How does annual percentage rate differ from interest rate?

Which is better, a 9 percent, fixed-rate loan for 30 years with payment of one point plus a half-percent origination fee, or an adjustable-rate mortgage for 20 years, currently at 6 percent, with four points up front?

It's like comparing apples and oranges.

First, of course, you must decide whether you have a gambler's instinct and will enjoy tracking interest rates and taking a chance on future payments being higher or lower than they were at the start. If rates are currently at the lower end of their inevitable cycle, however, you might prefer a fixed-rate loan. But trying to compare rates on such different mortgage plans, with varying closing costs, is very difficult.

To aid the consumer, lenders are required to quote an annual percentage rate (APR), which takes into account points and certain closing costs.

Suppose you do pay 6 percent, but with four extra points in a lump sum at closing. Clearly, your rate is really more than 6 percent. It's not six plus four because you pay those four points only once, not every year. But it's more than six. How much more? That's the APR. Not all lenders calculate it the same way, but it is useful for comparison shopping.

55. What's a conventional mortgage?

Loans agreed upon between you and the lender, without any government intervention except for banking regulations, are known as *conventional mortgages*. Because banking theory holds that it is unsafe to lend more than 80 percent of the value of a property, the standard conventional loan requires 20 percent down. With a 20 percent down payment, you have an 80 percent loan-to-value (LTV) ratio.

If you put down less than 20 percent on a conventional loan, you will be asked to carry private mortgage insurance (PMI). This insurance, for which you pay a small premium, has nothing to do with life or health insurance. Instead, it protects the lending institution in case the loan goes sour and the property can't be sold for enough to cover the debt. Because this lessens the lender's risk, you can sometimes borrow with as little as 5 percent down (a 95 percent LTV ratio).

56. How do adjustable-rate mortgages work?

Until the early 1980s, almost all mortgages were fixed-rate loans, with a borrower knowing in advance exactly what the monthly payment would run for principal and interest over the full 15, 25 or 30 years of the loan.

As interest rates began to skyrocket and finally hit 18 percent, lenders found themselves locked into unprofitable long-term commitments to keep their money lent out at rates like 5, 6 and 7 percent. This led to serious problems for lending institutions, and many were reluctant to make any further fixed-interest loans.

What emerged was the adjustable-rate mortgage, the ARM. The ARM shifts the risk of rising interest rates to the borrower, who also stands to benefit if rates drop during the loan period. An ARM is often chosen when interest rates are high; when rates drop, most borrowers prefer to lock in fixed-rate loans. Those who plan to remain in a house for only a short time may opt for an ARM that starts low and won't be adjusted for three, five or even seven years.

In order to choose wisely, the borrower must shop around, asking about the details of each ARM to find the one best suited to his or her situation.

Judging adjustable-rate mortgages requires an understanding of a whole new vocabulary.

Index. The interest rate on your loan may go up or down, following the trend for interest rates across the country.

To keep things fair, your lender must key the changes to some national indicator of current rates. The indicator must be outside the control of your lender, and it should be a figure you can check for yourself, as published in the business sections of newspapers.

The most commonly chosen indexes are the rates at which investors currently lend money to the government through purchase of U.S. Treasury notes and bills. The index used for your ARM might be the rate on sales of one-year, three-year or five-year Treasury obligations.

Margin.   If Treasury bills are the chosen index, and they sell at 6 percent interest, for example, your lender will not make mortgage loans at that rate. Rather, you will pay a specific percentage above the index.

If you are offered a 2 percent margin, you would pay 8 percent. If, at the time of interest adjustment, Treasury bills had gone to 7 percent, a 2 percent margin would set your mortgage rate at 9 percent. If they had dropped to 5.5 percent, your interest would drop to 7.5 percent.

Cap.   The word is used in two ways. First, your loan agreement may set, for example, a 2 percent cap on any upward adjustment. If interest rates (as reflected by your index) had gone up 3 percent by the time of adjustment, your rate could be raised only 2 percent.

When choosing an ARM, ask what happens in the above example. Is the extra 1 percent saved to be used for "catch-up" at the next adjustment, even though interest rates might have remained level? Or will you have negative amortization (see below)?

The second use of the word is synonymous with *ceiling*.

Ceiling.   A ceiling (sometimes called a lifetime cap) is an interest rate beyond which your loan can never go. Typically, you may be offered a five-point ceiling. This means that if your loan starts at 8 percent, it can never go beyond 13 percent, no matter what happens to national interest rates. A ceiling allows you to calculate your worst case.

Worst Case.   If your 30-year adjustable loan for $85,000 now costs $510 a month for principal and interest at 6 percent, and if your ceiling is 5 percent, the worst that could ever happen is that your interest rate would go to 11 percent. You can and should calculate in advance what the worst case could cost you—$809 a month.

Negative Amortization.   Regular amortization involves the gradual paying down of the principal borrowed, through part of your monthly payments. If, however, your monthly payments don't cover even the interest due, negative amortization is a possibility.

Suppose that interest on your loan should total $700 a month. For some reason, however, your monthly payment is set at $650. The shortfall, $50 a month, may be added to the amount you have borrowed. At the end of the year, you'd owe not less but about $600 more than when you started.

Negative amortization could result from an artificially low initial interest rate, or it could follow a hike in rates larger than your cap allows the lender to impose.

Not all mortgage plans include the possibility of negative amortization. Sometimes the lender agrees to absorb any shortfalls. But you should ask whether negative amortization is a possibility, and in what fashion, before choosing a specific ARM.

Convertibility.   If your mortgage offers this attractive feature, you have the best of both worlds. You can convert your adjustable-rate mortgage to a fixed-rate loan if you'd like.

With some plans, you can seize any favorable time (when fixed rates are generally low) during the life of the mortgage; more commonly, you can make the choice on certain anniversaries of the loan. Cash outlay for the conversion is low compared with the costs of placing a completely new mortgage; one point, or 1 percent of the loan, is typical. Be sure to inquire what the conversion would cost. You may, however, pay a slightly higher interest rate all along, in return for the option. And be sure you understand what rate you'd be able to convert to. Often it, too, is slightly higher than whatever rate the lender offers at that time.

Initial Interest Rate.   With most ARMs, the rate during the first year, or the first adjustment period, is set artificially low to induce a borrower to enter into an agreement—a "teaser" or "come-on" rate. Buyers who plan to be in a house for only a few years may be delighted with such arrangements, especially if no interest adjustment is planned for some years. Other borrowers, however, may end up with negative amortization and payment shock.

The prudent borrower asks the lender, "If you were not offering this initially low rate, what would my true interest be today? If things remained exactly the same, what rate (and what dollar amount) would I pay after the first adjustment period?"

Payment Shock.   The borrower who starts out with an artificially low rate may easily carry the payments. Suppose, however, that the rate eventually rises to the full ceiling allowed. The result would be a bad attack of payment shock leading—in some cases—to foreclosure and loss of the property. After many bad experiences, most lenders require borrowers to qualify to carry the payments at next year's rate, even if this year's is low.

Adjustment Period.   This is the length of time between interest rate adjustments. Typically made at the end of each year, adjustments might also be made as often as every six months or as infrequently as every seven years.

With some loans, interest rates may be adjusted even if monthly payments are not. This could result in negative amortization or, if rates have declined while payments have not, in faster reduction of the principal owed.

Principal.   This is the amount you borrowed; the amount remaining on the debt at any given time.

Buydown.   Extra, up-front, lump-sum payment of interest may bring down the interest rate charged on a loan. In some cases, the lower rate lasts for the whole life of the loan. In a 3-2-1 buydown, however, interest is reduced 3 percent for the first year of the loan, 2 percent the next year and 1 percent the third year. After that, interest reaches normal levels. Any plan offering a lower interest rate in return for more up-front points is, in effect, a buydown.

57. Should I take a 15-year or 30-year loan?

Thirty-year mortgage loans have been losing some popularity to 20-year and even 15-year mortgages. Monthly payments on a 15-year loan can run about 20 percent higher than on the same loan figured on a 30-year basis. You would need about 20 percent more income to qualify for the shorter loan. On the other hand, you'd make payments only half as long and cut your total interest cost considerably.

The 15-year mortgage operates like enforced savings because it requires you to pay off the debt faster. It may be appropriate if, for example, your children will start college in 15 years, at a time when you'd like to own your home free and clear.

The shorter mortgage term does tie up your money, however. If you have the discipline, there's nothing to stop you from putting that extra money, each month, into your own savings account, where you can tap it as needed and where it will earn extra interest.

58. Are there income tax advantages to a larger mortgage?

It never makes sense to borrow money and pay interest just to get an income tax deduction. If you can choose whether to make a large down payment or a small one, whether to borrow more or less, base your decision on your total financial situation, your age, how long you plan to stay in the home and similar factors. Ignore the tax aspects of the decision.

59. Do biweekly payments really work magic, or are they just hocus-pocus?

Some mortgage plans involve biweekly mortgage payments, with half a monthly payment automatically deducted from your checking or savings account every two weeks. The results seem like magic to many borrowers because they can't help thinking of it as half a payment twice a month. Biweekly isn't twice a month at all. In some months, you might make a payment on the first, the fifteenth and then the twenty-ninth.

Paying every two weeks adds up to 26 half-payments a year, the equivalent of 13 payments instead of 12 each year. It's that extra thirteenth payment that does the trick, cutting the length of a 30-year mortgage to 21 years or less.

Many lenders do not offer biweekly payment plans, but outside companies do. If you join up, usually for about $400, the company will automatically deduct half a month's payment from your bank account every two weeks and forward your regular payments on your existing mortgage monthly. Once a year, having collected that thirteenth payment, the company will send it to your lender with instructions that it be used as an extra reduction of your principal.

There's nothing to stop you from accomplishing the same thing on your own.

If you have the discipline, you can achieve the same results simply by making extra principal payments directly to your lender. One caution: be sure to check your statements to make sure the additional money is properly credited, not just stashed in your escrow account. If your mortgage company does not send monthly statements, it owes you at least a full year's review each January.

It's easy to figure how much extra payments will save you. If you pay 9 percent on your loan, for example, and you send in an extra $5,000 to be applied to the principal, from that point on you are borrowing $5,000 less than scheduled and saving $450 a year in interest. The effects of compounding and income tax deductions affect that calculation but not significantly.

And, of course, you'll pay off the loan months before it was originally scheduled to end.

60. Do you recommend using an FHA mortgage?

The Federal Housing Authority (FHA), an agency of the Department of Housing and Urban Development (HUD), was established to help homeowners buy with low down payments. Lenders can safely make loans of up to 97 percent of the value of property because the FHA insures them against loss in case of foreclosure.

If FHA loans are used in your area, they can be a fine way to borrow. The money comes not from the government but from local lenders, so if none in your locality handles FHA mortgages, you're out of luck. The loans are not intended for expensive property, but upper limits in high-price areas are raised from time to time. In 1995, the maximum FHA loan was $151,725; in low-cost counties, it was $77,197.

For inexpensive property (less than $50,000), down payment can be as little as 3 percent; in any case, it runs less than 5 percent. FHA loans may be placed on one-family to four-family dwellings and are intended for owner-occupants.

Insurance premiums (to protect the lender in case of default) are due in a lump sum at closing and can run up to 2.25 percent of the loan. Because most FHA buyers don't have extra cash at closing, the mortgage insurance premium (MIP) can be added to the amount of the mortgage loan. If you pay off your FHA mortgage within the first few years, a portion of your MIP is returned. In addition to the one-time MIP, you'll pay 0.5 percent of the outstanding balance each year. The number of years this additional premium is charged depends on the size of the down payment; minimum-down loans require the extra charge over the longest period.

61. Does the FHA inspection of the property protect me?

Somewhat.

The FHA bases its loans on the value found by authorized FHA appraisers and sometimes requires certain repairs (items dealing with the preservation of the property and with health and safety) before the loan will be granted. If the FHA inspector misses anything, though, you have no recourse against the FHA or HUD.

In addition to the standard FHA program, #203-b, others are available in certain areas. FHA 203-k, for example, lends money to cover both the cost of a home in need of substantial rehabilitation and the money needed for repairs.

Your real estate broker will know whether any of these programs is available in your community—or you can sit down with the yellow pages open to "Mortgages" and spend a couple of hours calling around yourself. If FHA loans are not handled locally, you can talk with a mortgage broker about whether your mortgage could be placed elsewhere.

62. What's so great about VA mortgages?

The most attractive thing about VA loans is the possibility of no down payment. In addition, a cooperative seller (if you can locate one) is allowed to furnish some or all of your closing costs and even the prepaid taxes and insurance required at closing. You could conceivably buy without using a cent of your own money. No subsidy is involved, however, and you must qualify to carry the payments as you would with any other mortgage.

VA loans may be used for one-family to four-family homes, owner-occupied only. They are assumable (according to the restrictions listed in the discussion of assumptions).

As with FHA mortgages, the money comes from a local lender; the Department of Veterans Affairs contribution is to guarantee the loan at no cost to the veteran. While FHA loans require low down payments, VA loans may be made for the entire appraised value of the property (a 100 percent LTV ratio). In 1995, the VA would guarantee loans as high as $203,100.

63. Who qualifies for a VA mortgage?

For a VA-guaranteed loan, the veteran needs a discharge "other than dishonorable" and one of the following:

- 180 days' active (not reserve) duty between September 16, 1940, and September 7, 1980
- 90 days' service during a war (the Korean, Vietnam and Gulf conflicts are considered wars)
- Six years' service in the reserves or National Guard
- Two years' service after September 7, 1980

In-service VA mortgages are also possible.

Eligibility for such mortgages does not expire. If one's first VA loan is paid off, full eligibility is regained.

At closing, a funding fee is paid directly to the Department of Veterans Affairs.

64. Are there any mortgages with subsidized payments?

In rural areas, direct mortgage loans can sometimes be obtained from the Rural Economic and Community Development Administration (formerly the Farmers Home Administration or FmHA). If your income falls within specific limits (fairly low, depending on family size), you can buy a modest home on no more than one acre, with interest payments tailored to your income.

The program is intended for those who cannot obtain financing elsewhere. The money is allotted to local offices quarterly. At any given time, some offices will have money available; others will have waiting lists. The FmHA processes mortgage applications before you've found a house, then notifies you as money becomes available.

At any given time, various other programs are offered by states or municipalities to build up their housing stock or to help first-time buyers get into the market. It's always worth calling your town or city hall to inquire whether there's something offered that would be of value to you. Brokers usually stay informed on local programs and on the loans offered through most of the states.

65. Would an assumable mortgage help me?

An assumable mortgage is one that can remain with the property when it is sold. This results in considerable savings for the next buyer, with no outlay for the costs associated with placing a new mortgage—items like appraisal of the property, mortgage tax and the like.

A high assumable mortgage, or one at a low interest rate, is therefore worth a premium and contributes extra value to property on the market.

FHA loans made before December 1, 1986, and VA loans made before March 1, 1988, are completely—freely—assumable. This means that you, or anyone the seller chooses, can take the loan along with the real estate, just as it stands. Neither you nor the home need pass any evaluation by the lending institution, which has no say in the matter. Closing costs are negligible, the interest rate will not change and the transaction can be closed, or settled, as soon as the parties wish.

In areas where prices have risen, of course, these older loans represent only part of the property value. You must pay the seller the rest of the purchase price in cash unless you can persuade the owner to take back financing. The seller who does so agrees to hold a second mortgage for part of the purchase price, or even—in rare instances—for the entire missing amount (requiring no money down!)

You'd have to look pretty good financially before a seller would enter into such an arrangement because even though you take over the payments on the loan and ownership of the property, the seller retains liability for that FHA or VA debt if anything goes wrong.

Newer FHA and VA loans are classified as "assumable with bank approval." To take over a more recent FHA mortgage, you must prove qualification (income and credit) to the lending institution's satisfaction. Once that's done, if you make the payments promptly, the original borrower retains liability for only five years. With newer VA mortgages, the person assuming the loan (who need not be a veteran) must qualify with the lender before any assumption occurs. A charge of no more than $500 may be made for the paperwork.

Besides FHA and VA loans, many adjustable-rate mortgages have assumability features, which allow for considerable savings on closing costs. ARM mortgages differ; most stipulate that the new borrower must qualify with the lender and that the interest rate may be adjusted upon assumption. Some charge is made for the privilege; one point might be typical.

66. Where else can I find mortgage money?

A seller may agree to hold financing, lending you money on a first mortgage or, if the property already has one, on a second (typically shorter term) loan.

A family member may agree to lend you part of the purchase price, in which case it is prudent to keep things on a business-like basis, offering the property as security for a regular mortgage. Doing so also will allow you an income tax deduction for interest paid. If the property is not pledged, you'd pay nondeductible interest on a simple personal loan.

Family members may offer low-interest or no-interest loans, but the Internal Revenue Service takes a dim view of them. It likes to see a private mortgage loan made at either 9 percent or the "applicable federal rate," an index published monthly by the government that follows current trends in interest rates. If the mortgage rate does not meet that standard, the IRS will *impute* the interest and tax the lender as if it had been received.

67. What's the difference between a land contract and a lease option?

A *land contract* (contract for deed, contract sale) is a type of layaway installment plan for buying a home. Typically, it is sought by a buyer who does not have enough down payment to qualify for a bank loan or to persuade the seller to turn over title (ownership). You move in, make monthly payments to the seller and take care of taxes, insurance and repairs, exactly as if you owned the place. But title does not transfer to you until a specified time, perhaps when you make the final payment. With some land contracts, you receive title when you have made enough payments to constitute 20 percent equity. *Equity* is defined as the amount you "have in" the property—roughly, market value minus debt owed. Often the expectation is that you will qualify for a regular mortgage loan along the way and pay off the land contract.

A *lease option* differs from a land contract in that you are not bound to buy the property. Instead, you move in as a tenant and typically pay a nonrefundable flat amount, perhaps $1,000 or $2,000 in return for an option—the right to purchase at a given price within a given time (typically one, two or three years). If you decide not to buy, you simply remain as a tenant for the duration of the lease. Who pays for what expenses and whether any of your rent goes toward the purchase price are negotiable.

Any land contract or lease option requires extra careful consultation with your attorney before you sign anything. Such contracts can vary considerably in their provisions, and you must have someone on your side making sure your interests are protected. Either type of contract should be recorded—that is, entered in the public records to notify the world at large of your rights in the property.

68. Should I stay away from a balloon mortgage?

Not necessarily, but you'd better understand exactly how it works.

Suppose an 80-year-old seller is ready to take back a $100,000 mortgage on the house you are buying from him. It might be because the house could not meet bank standards and he is unable to make the necessary repairs; it might be because he'd prefer regular monthly income to a lump sum; it might be because your unusual circumstances (for example, you're just starting your own business) don't let you qualify for a bank loan.

At that age, the seller doesn't like the idea of making a 30-year loan (not realizing that he could simply leave the remainder of the mortgage to his heirs). He will be comfortable only if he will see all his money within ten years.

But if you pay at the proper rate for a ten-year loan, your monthly payments will be more than you can handle. So you offer the seller a *balloon* mortgage. Your payments—principal and interest—will be calculated as if you were paying on a 30-year schedule. But at the end of ten years, whatever you still owe will immediately become all due and payable.

Because during the early years of a loan most of the monthly payment goes for interest, you will not reduce the principal much over those ten years. You will still owe about 90 percent of the original loan. That final balloon payment will be a big one. A five-year balloon mortgage is sometimes referred to as "sixty and surprise"—the surprise being that big 61st payment.

The usual plan is that your finances will have straightened out, you will have built up equity (the money you've paid off plus any increase in property value) and the house will have been repaired, and you can now place a mortgage with a regular lending institution. Or the old gentleman may still be in good health, and so dependent on your prompt and regular checks that he agrees to renew the loan.

69. How do I finance the construction of a new home?

Financing new construction is easiest if you work with a large builder, who may finance the construction or help you arrange a building loan that later converts to a mortgage. If you buy your own building lot, you will find banks reluctant to lend on vacant land. You'll have to buy for cash or persuade the seller to hold a mortgage.

Once the land is paid for, you can count it toward equity to help qualify for another loan. A building loan is most readily obtained after you have taken all the necessary steps in having your plans and lot approved by local authorities and if you are working through a recognized contractor. Do-it-yourselfers, particularly those on a shoestring, find it very difficult to obtain financing.

Chapter 9

*N*egotiating for Your Dream Home

*A*fter you've located your dream home, the next step is to negotiate a contract for buying it.

The process resembles a tennis game. The homeowner made the first serve, a public offer to sell the property at a given price. Now the ball is in your court.

Local customs differ, particularly in the areas around New York and other large cities, which use a system of offers and bids, with the final contract written by attorneys.

In most localities, however, you start things off with an offer to buy, which includes not only price but many other provisions. The document you present to the seller is a written purchase offer. When the seller accepts it exactly as you presented it, it becomes a binding contract, which may be known in your community as a *deposit receipt,* a *contract of sale* or an *agreement to buy and sell.*

All real estate contracts must be in writing in order to be enforceable. (Translation: "Oral agreements aren't worth the paper they're written on.") If, in front of 20 witnesses, the homeowners said they were willing to sell you the property for $150,000 cash and took your deposit check, you still could not legally hold them to it.

The written contract supersedes any oral agreements. If the seller promises to leave the refrigerator, for example, make sure the contract mentions it, or you could be out of luck.

70. Who draws up my offer?

Depending on local custom, a broker or an attorney will usually help draw up a written purchase offer detailing the terms under which you propose to buy. In some areas, this is a full-fledged contract, needing only the seller's acceptance to be complete. Elsewhere, local custom may employ a preliminary memorandum, articles of agreement, a binder or a deposit receipt.

Can you draw up the offer for yourself? Yes, and you could perform your own surgery, too. In either case, it would be fine unless you happened to make an amateurish mistake. There's no use copying someone else's contract or a model; yours will differ in many respects according to the needs of the parties involved, local custom and state law. Brokers and lawyers must take courses, pass exams and gain related experience before they're allowed to fill out these forms. Don't try to do it yourself.

Ask the broker with whom you work for a copy of the purchase offer that is most common, or obtain a copy of the contract generally used by your Multiple Listing Service or bar association. Study it at leisure in advance because when it comes time to fill one in and sign it, you'll probably be too nervous for quiet consideration.

71. What price should I offer?

Before you begin negotiations and before emotions take over, settle in your mind the top price you really would invest in the house—a figure you should not share with the agent unless it is someone you specifically hired as your own broker.

Should you expect to pay full asking price, or is there a formula for the amount of bargaining built in by the seller?

The answer is simple: It all depends.

Homeowners who hate haggling may list their house at rock-bottom prices with no room for flexibility. Others may add a 5 percent cushion to what they'd really take.

The seller's circumstances also affect price. An owner may be under some of the pressures mentioned in the last chapter. Elderly homeowners, on the other hand, are often in no hurry to move. They may have emotional ties that make it difficult for them to view their property impartially.

If a house has been on the market a long time (more than five months), the buying public has voted that it isn't worth what the seller asks. In that case, don't offer full price.

On the other hand, don't drag your feet if you stumble on a hot listing, one that has just come on the market and is uniquely appealing or underpriced. If there is a possibility of several offers within the next day, consider bidding somewhat more than the asking price. This gives you an advantage over any competition. It often sounds suspicious when a broker recommends such action, however; this is where it helps if you already know and trust the agent.

72. What are comparables?

When you house hunt intensively in a given area, you quickly become an expert on homes that fall within your price range. You can recognize a bargain when it comes on the market. You also can spot overpriced property. For a short time, you may know more than anyone else in the world about the proper price for a three-bedroom ranch in Milkwood.

In an unfamiliar area, ask the agent for sales prices of comparables (comps). These are similar homes in the neighborhood that have recently changed hands; they'll give you something to judge by. Comparables, in fact, are the principal tool brokers themselves use to appraise property for market value. Other considerations in making price comparisons include the condition of the house, time of year, special financing available and the general economic climate—whether it's a buyers' or sellers' market.

Remember that the seller's broker may furnish comps but is not supposed to suggest that you offer anything less than the listed price. If you have hired your own buyer's broker, you can expect advice on the lowest price that might take the house.

You may be curious about what the homeowners paid three years ago for the place you want to buy today, but that is not relevant. If they had received it as a gift, must they then give it away? Or, on the other hand, if they've invested $25,000 in a gold-plated bathroom, are you then obliged to reimburse them? Of course not.

How much money the sellers have invested in the property and how much they need to get out of it are their concerns, not yours. In the end, runs the professional appraiser's maxim, "buyers make value." Selling price is set by the operation of supply and demand, in competition on the open market.

Your offering price will be affected by the terms under which you expect to buy. If the sellers must wait around while you market your present home, they'll be less inclined to drop their price. The same applies if they must come up with a cash payment of points to your lender. By the same token, a clean offer with no contingencies may be worth a price concession.

After price, the next big item in the contract is how you will finance your purchase. If you will assume a present loan or place your mortgage with the seller, these terms are detailed. You'll stipulate that the mortgage you take over must be current (paid up to date) at the time of transfer.

73. What are contingencies in a contract?

If you must obtain outside financing, the details of your proposed mortgage are spelled out, along with a statement that the contract is "contingent upon" or "subject to" your obtaining the loan. If you cannot find financing at the specific interest rate you have stipulated in the offer, you couldn't be required to go through with the purchase. The contract should state that in such a case, your deposit would be returned.

There may be other contingencies (happenings) that must be satisfied before you will buy. You may need to sell your present home, or obtain the job you came to town to interview for, or receive a satisfactory (to you) engineer's report. Any of these conditions would be inserted into the contract.

The sellers probably will be nervous about contingent offers. They will take their house off the market in your behalf, without any guarantee the sale will go through. So it's customary to set a time limit on contingencies. The contract might state that it is "contingent upon the buyer receiving a satisfactory engineer's report on the property within three days of acceptance of this offer" or "contingent upon approval by the buyer's husband when he arrives in town before next Saturday, September 11, at 6 PM"

For longer contingencies, particularly those involving the sale of your present house, the sellers may envision waiting around forever. Instead of worrying about the sale of their home, the seller must now worry about yours, over which they have even less control.

So it's only fair to insert an escape clause, or a kick-out. The wording may differ according to local practice, but the escape clause usually gives the seller the right to continue to show the house. If another good offer comes in, you may be required to remove the contingency and make your offer firm or else drop out.

If your contingency is called, you don't have to meet anyone else's offering price; your deal has been nailed down. But you would have to agree, for example, to buy the property whether or not you sell your present home. Otherwise, you could drop out and regain your deposit.

74. What property can I expect will be left with the house?

It is essential to spell out all the gray-area items (carpeting, fireplace equipment, chandeliers, drapes) about which there may be disputes as to whether they stay with the property.

In general, personal property that can be picked up and moved without leaving any nail or screw holes may be taken by the seller. The rules are complicated, though, and it's best to stipulate in the contract that "stove and refrigerator are to remain" or that "seller may remove dining room chandelier."

Items like wall-to-wall carpeting, wood stoves, swing sets and satellite dishes are subject to occasional differences of opinion; head off trouble by detailing them in the written offer. If the listing agent did a proper job, the sellers will already have indicated which items they are taking or leaving. Ask the broker to do some delicate investigating about the sellers' plans for the above-ground pool or the tool shed.

Don't get bogged down over small items. Just make sure your offer specifies what you expect to remain. Don't discuss furniture or rugs you might like to buy at this point; wait until you have a firm purchase contract.

75. What else belongs in my offer?

It's a good idea to stipulate that you have the right to inspect the premises within 24 hours before closing. You will want to make sure the seller left the fireplace tools or removed the piles of magazines in the attic.

Also necessary in the contract are a target date and place for transfer of title. Choose a date that will allow for processing of your mortgage application; the agent will have suggestions.

What if that date comes and goes? You still have a binding contract. If a certain deadline is absolutely essential, you can use the powerful legal phrase "time is of the essence," but this is strong medicine; don't do it without consulting your lawyer.

Experience has taught agents and lawyers to provide for all sorts of complications that may not have occurred to you. What if the place burns down before closing? If the bank's appraiser thinks the property isn't worth the price you're paying? If taxes weren't paid last year? If the sellers can't prove they have clear title (ownership)? If a full tank of oil remains in the basement? Will you receive occupancy on the day you settle? Will you receive a full warranty deed, or does local custom use a lesser deed?

All these questions should be answered in a well-drawn contract.

You will set a time limit on your offer, and it should be a short one. A day or two is enough time for the sellers to consider your proposal. If you give them more time, they may be tempted to stall until after they see what next Sunday's open house might bring. They might also use your offer as an auction goad to bid up another prospective buyer. If the sellers are out of town, they should be available by phone and could answer your offer by fax, with a confirming letter to follow.

76. Must I make an earnest money deposit?

An offer to buy is usually accompanied by a substantial deposit, variously known as *binder* or *earnest money*. This sum serves several purposes. It proves to the sellers that you mean business. They are, after all, going to take the property off the market on your behalf. The deposit also serves as a source of damages if you back out for no good reason a month down the line. The deposit is usually placed with a broker or an attorney, who deposits it in a separate escrow, or trust, account. Avoid giving the deposit directly to the seller.

You may be told that 6 percent or 10 percent of the purchase price is necessary. If this is inconvenient, insist that you can come up with only a smaller amount. Remember, though, that the sellers are weighing your offer to see whether it will result in a successful sale. Without much earnest money, it may not look convincing.

This earnest money, of course, counts toward the sum you'll need at closing. It doesn't add to your costs. Your full deposit is credited toward the down payment or other settlement expenses. The contract should clearly state under what circumstances the earnest money may be returned.

77. What legal problems could I run into?

The contract provides that you will receive clear title, full unchallenged control and ownership, except for certain liens and easements that are spelled out. These are claims that third parties may have against the property. You agree to take possession even though the telephone company has the right to run wires through the backyard or a neighbor has the right to share the driveway; these are known as *easements of record*. You don't agree to be responsible for unknown liens (financial claims) that turn up later, like an unpaid roofing bill or an outstanding home-improvement loan.

It's reassuring to take the contract to your lawyer before you sign it. But many sales are made after office hours and on weekends, and you may risk losing the right house if you delay. In this case, you can write above your signature "subject to the approval in form of my attorney." This means that you can go ahead and make your offer, while reserving for your lawyer the right to object later to any wording or provisions that don't protect your interests. The lawyer can even disapprove the whole contract.

Most lawyers refuse to give advice on price, feeling this is out of their field of expertise. The attorney's job is to see that the contract protects you and accomplishes your objectives. You can safely follow local custom about who writes an uncomplicated contract.

78. What happens after I sign the offer?

Although local customs vary, in most areas the broker will present your offer to the seller, with you not present. You'll be advised to go home and wait by the phone. The agent, meanwhile, may contact the listing broker and the seller to arrange for presentation of the offer as soon as possible; prompt forwarding of all offers is one of the broker's primary legal responsibilities. No broker has the right to refuse to convey a written offer, no matter how small.

The tennis game is on, and the next move is the seller's. The response can be "yes" (acceptance), "no" (refusal) or "maybe" (counteroffer).

If it's yes, the seller accepts all your terms, and you have a binding contract. You can skip the rest of this chapter!

If it's no, the homeowners cannot later change their minds and get your offer back (unless you agree).

Then there's maybe. A good negotiator will bring you a counteroffer rather than a rejection: "We accept all terms and conditions except that the purchase price shall be $183,000 and we'll throw in the stove and refrigerator."

The seller is now bound by the counteroffer, which probably contains a time limit, while you are free to consider its terms. You may want to counter the counteroffer, perhaps split the difference.

Too many volleys, though, result in hard feelings and often kill the deal. People begin to say, "It's not the money, it's the principle of the thing." Instead of working together toward what is legally known as a *meeting of the minds,* buyer and seller start to see the negotiation as a war. They concentrate on winning and lose sight of their original goals.

Before you begin negotiating, make up your mind that you will not lose the home you really want over the last thousand dollars. When you cannot make any further concessions on price, try to include some face-saving gesture toward the seller: "I can't go any higher, but I'll move the closing date for your convenience."

Make your first offer, certainly your second one, close to the top price you'd really pay. The idea is to tempt the sellers to wrap up the deal, even if it isn't quite what they had in mind.

79. Can I forget the whole thing if I don't like the counteroffer?

At each stage, the person who made the last proposal is bound by it until the offer is withdrawn or answered. The game ends when one side accepts unconditionally the other's last offer—or drops out.

Remember that if your proposal is accepted, you will have a binding legal contract. Don't fool around with a purchase offer unless you really want to buy the property. It should be a thrill when you finally receive the notification of acceptance that is the final legal requirement to make a contract binding: "Congratulations! They said yes. You've just bought a home!"

PURCHASE AND SALE CONTRACT
FOR RESIDENTIAL PROPERTY

Plain English Form published by and only for use of members of the Greater Rochester Association of Realtors, Inc. and the Monroe County Bar Association. **COMMISSIONS OR FEES FOR THE REAL ESTATE SERVICES TO BE PROVIDED ARE NEGOTIABLE BETWEEN REALTOR AND CLIENT. When Signed, This Document Becomes A Binding Contract. Buyer or Seller May Wish To Consult Their Own Attorney.**

TO: _____

_____ (Seller) FROM: _____ (Buyer)

OFFER TO PURCHASE

Buyer offers to purchase the property described below from Seller on the following terms:

1. PROPERTY DESCRIPTION.

Property known as No. _____ in the (Town) (City) (Village) of _____ State of New York, also

known as Tax No. _____ including all buildings and any other improvements and all rights which the Seller has in or with the property.

Approximate Lot Size: _____ (Check if applicable) [ ] As described in more detail in the attached description.

Description of Buildings on Property: _____

2. OTHER ITEMS INCLUDED IN PURCHASE. The following items, if any, now in or on the property are included in this purchase and sale. All heating, plumbing, septic and private water systems, lighting fixtures, flowers, shrubs, trees, window shades and blinds, curtain and traverse rods, storm windows, storm doors, screens, awnings, TV antennae, water softeners, sump pumps, window boxes, mail box, tool shed, fences, underground pet containment fencing with control devices, wall-to-wall carpeting and runners, exhaust fans, hoods, garbage disposal, electric garage door opener and remote control devices, intercom equipment, humidifier, security systems, smoke detectors, all fireplace screens and enclosures, swimming pool and all related equipment and accessories, and the following, if built-in: cabinets, mirrors, stoves, ovens, dishwashers, trash compactors, shelving and air conditioning (except window units). Buyer agrees to accept these items in their present conditions. Other items to be included in the purchase and sale are: _____

[ ] Seller represents to the best of Seller's knowledge that any heating, plumbing, air conditioning, electrical systems and included appliances are presently in good working order, except for

_____

Items not included are: _____

Seller represents that he has good title to all of the above items to be transferred to Buyer, and will deliver a Bill of Sale for the same at closing.

3. PRICE: AMOUNT AND HOW IT WILL BE PAID: The purchase price is _____ Dollars

$ _____, Buyer shall receive credit at closing for any deposit made hereunder. The balance of the purchase price shall be paid as follows: (Check and complete applicable provisions.)

[ ] (a) Seller agrees to pay a loan fee of _____ % of the mortgage amount.

[ ] (b) All in cash, or certified check at closing.

[ ] (c) By Buyer assuming and agreeing to pay according to its terms, the principal balance of the mortgage in the approximate amount of $_____ provided that the mortgage is assumable without the holder's approval. Buyer held by _____ which includes principal, understands that the mortgage bears interest at the rate of _____% per year and the monthly payments are $_____. Buyer agrees to pay the interest, taxes and insurance (strike out any item not included in payment), with the last payment due on approximately _____ 19/20_____. Buyer understands that principal balance may be lower at time of closing because balance of the purchase price over the amount of the assumed mortgage in cash or certified check at closing. If the mortgage to be assumed provides for graduated or balloon payments, then a copy of the original bond and mortgage shall be of monthly payments made after this contract is signed. If the mortgage to be assumed provides for graduated or balloon payments, then a copy of the original bond and mortgage shall be furnished to Buyer's attorney for approval within ten days after acceptance of this offer.

[ ] (d) By Buyer delivering a purchase money bond and mortgage to Seller at closing. This purchase money bond and mortgage shall be in the amount of $_____ shall be amortized over a term of _____ years from the date of closing, shall bear interest at the rate of _____% per year, and shall be paid in monthly installments of $_____ including principal and interest. The mortgage shall contain the statutory clauses as to payment, insurance, acceleration on default of thirty days, taxes, assessments, and water rates and also shall provide for late charges of 2% of any monthly payment which is not paid within 15 days after it is due and for recovery of reasonable attorney's fees if the mortgage is foreclosed.

The mortgage shall allow Buyer to prepay all or part of the mortgage without penalty at any time but shall also provide that the mortgage be paid in full if Buyer sells the property, unless Seller consents in writing to assumption of the mortgage debt. The balance of the purchase price will be paid at closing in cash, or certified check.

4. CONTINGENCIES. Buyer makes this offer subject to the following contingencies. If any of these contingencies is not satisfied by the dates specified, then either Buyer or Seller may cancel this contract by written notice to the other. (Check and complete applicable provisions.)

[ ] (a) **Mortgage Contingency.** This offer subject to Buyer obtaining and accepting a _____ mortgage loan commitment in an amount not to exceed _____ at an interest rate not to exceed _____%, for a term of _____ years. Buyer shall immediately apply for this loan and shall have until _____ to obtain and accept a written mortgage commitment. The conditions of any such mortgage commitment shall not be deemed contingencies of this contract but shall be the sole responsibility of Buyer. If the loan commitment requires repairs, replacements, or improvements to be made or painting to be done, before closing, then Seller shall do the work and install the materials and improvements needed or have the same done, at Seller's expense. However, if the cost of doing so exceeds $_____ Seller shall not be obligated to have such work done, and Buyer will be allowed either to receive credit at closing for the amount recited above and incur any necessary expenses to comply with the loan commitment requirements, or to cancel this contract by written notice to Seller, and any deposit shall be returned to Buyer. Issuance and acceptance by the Buyer of a written mortgage commitment shall be deemed a waiver and satisfaction of this contingency.

[ ] (b) **Mortgage Assumption Contingency.** This offer is subject to Buyer obtaining permission to assume the existing mortgage loan balance referred to above in (3c) by _____ 19_____. If the mortgage holder requires that the interest rate be increased for such approval to be given, Buyer agrees to assume the mortgage at such rate as long as it does not exceed _____%. at the time of the commitment. [ ] Buyer agrees to obtain a release of Seller's liability and to pay any assumption or release of liability fees.

[ ] (c) **Sale Contract Contingency.** This offer is subject to Buyer obtaining a contract for the sale of Buyer's property located at _____ no later than _____, 199_____. Unless and until Buyer has removed this sale contingency in writing, if Seller receives another acceptable purchase offer, Seller may notify Buyer in writing that Seller wants to accept the other offer and Buyer will then have _____ days to remove this sale contingency by written notice to the Seller. If Buyer does not remove this sale contingency after receiving notice from Seller, Buyer's rights under this contract shall end, and Seller shall be free to accept the other purchase offer and Buyer's deposit shall be returned. Buyer may not remove this sale contingency if Buyer's mortgage loan commitment requires the sale and transfer of this property as a condition of the mortgage loan funding, unless Buyer has a contract for the sale of this property which is not then subject to any unsatisfied contingencies.

[ ] (d) **Transfer of Title Contingency.** This offer is contingent upon the transfer of title to Buyer's property located at _____ no later than _____, 199_____. [ ] Buyer represents that Buyer has entered into a contract for sale of Buyer's property which is now subject to the following contingencies: [ ] None; [ ] Mortgage; [ ] Assumption of Mortgage; [ ] Sale of Property; [ ] Transfer of Title; [ ] Attorney Approval; and/or [ ] Other _____ Unless and until Buyer has obtained a contract for sale of Buyer's property which is not subject to any unsatisfied contingencies, and has so notified the Seller in writing, if Seller receives another acceptable purchase offer, Seller may notify Buyer in writing that Seller wants to accept the other offer and Buyer will then have _____ days to remove this transfer of title contingency by written notice to the Seller. If Buyer does not remove this transfer of title contingency after receiving notice from Seller, Buyer's rights under this contract shall end, and Seller shall be free to accept the other purchase offer and Buyer's deposit shall be returned. Buyer may not remove this transfer of title contingency if Buyer's mortgage loan commitment requires the sale and transfer of this property as a condition of the mortgage loan funding, unless Buyer has a contract for sale of this property which is not then subject to any unsatisfied contingencies.

[ ] (e) Attorney Approval. This contract is subject to the written approval of attorneys for Buyer and Seller within _____ days from date of acceptance (the "Approval Period"). If either attorney makes written objection to the contract within the Approval Period, and such objection is not cured by written approval by both attorneys and all of the parties within the Approval Period, then either Buyer or Seller may cancel this contract by written notice to the other and any deposit shall be returned to the Buyer.

[ ] (f) Waiver of Attorney Approval. This offer is not subject to the Buyer's attorney approval.

[ ] (g) Other Contingencies. _____

5. Closing Date and Place. Transfer of title shall take place at the _____ County Clerk's Office or at the offices of Buyer's lender on or before _____, 19_____ .

6. Buyer's Possession of Property.

[ ] Buyer shall have possession of the property on the day of closing, in broom clean condition, with all keys to the property delivered to Buyer at closing.

[ ] Seller shall have the right to retain possession for _____ days after closing at the cost of $_____ per day, plus utilities. At possession, the property shall be broom clean and all keys shall be delivered to Buyer.

7. Title Documents. Seller shall provide the following documents in connection with the sale:

A. Deed. Seller will deliver to Buyer at closing a properly signed and notarized Warranty Deed with lien covenant (or Executor's Deed, Administrator's Deed or Trustee's Deed, if Seller holds title as such).

B. Abstract, Bankruptcy and Tax Searches, and Instrument Survey Map. Seller will furnish and pay for and deliver to Buyer or Buyer's attorney at least 15 days prior to the date of closing, fully guaranteed tax, title and United States Court Searches dated or redated after the date of this contract with a local tax certificate for Village, or City taxes, if any, and an instrument survey map dated or redated after the date of this contract. Seller will pay for the map or redated map and for continuing such searches to and including the day of closing. Any survey map shall be prepared or redated and certified to meet the standards and requirements of Buyer's mortgage lender and of the Monroe County Bar Association.

8. Marketability of Title. The deed and other documents delivered by Seller shall be sufficient to convey good marketable title in fee simple, to the property free and clear of all liens and encumbrances. However, Buyer agrees to accept title to the property subject to restrictive covenants of record common to the tract or subdivision of which the property is a part, provided these restrictions have not been violated, or if they have been violated, that the time for anyone to complain of the violations has expired. Buyer also agrees to accept title to the property subject to public utility easements along lot lines as long as those easements do not interfere with any buildings now on the property or with any improvements Buyer may construct in compliance with all present restrictive covenants of record and zoning and building codes applicable to the Property. Seller agrees to furnish a smoke alarm affidavit at closing and to cooperate in executing any documents required by federal or state laws for transfer of title to residential property.

9. Objections to Title. If Buyer raises a valid written objection to Seller's title which means that the title to the property is unmarketable, and if Buyer makes a written request for it, Seller shall reimburse Buyer for the reasonable cost of having the title notice of cancellation to Buyer. Buyer's deposit shall be returned immediately, and if Buyer makes a written request for it, Seller shall reimburse Buyer for the reasonable cost of having the title examined. However, if Seller gives notice within 5 days that Seller will cure the problem prior to the closing date, or if the title objection is insurable and Buyer is willing to accept insurable title, then this contract shall continue in force until the closing date, subject to the Seller performing as promised and/or providing insurable title at Seller's expense. If Seller fails to cure the problem within such time, Buyer will not be obligated to purchase the property and Buyer's deposit shall be returned together with reimbursement for the reasonable cost of having the title examined.

10. Recording Costs, Mortgage Tax, Transfer Tax and Closing Adjustments. Seller will pay the real property transfer tax and special additional mortgage recording tax, if applicable. Buyer will pay mortgage assumption charges, if any, and will pay for recording the deed and the mortgage, and for mortgage tax. The following, as applicable, will be prorated and adjusted between Seller and Buyer as of the date of closing: current taxes computed on a fiscal year basis, excluding any delinquent items, interest and penalties; rent payments; fuel oil on the premises; water charges; pure water charges; sewer charges; mortgage interest; current common charges or assessments; prepaid F.H.A. Mortgage Insurance Premium (M.I.P.) of approximately $_____ with the exact amount to be calculated at closing in accordance with F.H.A. formulae. Any F.H.A. insurance premium which is not prepaid, but rather paid monthly, shall be adjusted at closing. If there is a water meter at the property, Seller shall furnish an actual reading to a date not more than thirty (30) days before the closing date set forth in this contract. At closing the water charges and any sewer rent shall be apportioned on the basis of such actual reading.

11. Zoning. Seller represents that the property is in full compliance with all zoning or building ordinances for use as a _____ . If applicable laws require it, the Seller will furnish at or before closing, a Certificate of Occupancy for the property, dated within ninety (90) days of the closing, with Seller completing the work and installing the materials and improvements needed to obtain Certificate of Occupancy. However, if the cost of obtaining a Certificate of Occupancy exceeds $_____, Seller shall not be obligated to have such work done, and Buyer will be allowed either to receive credit at closing for the amount recited above, and incur the necessary expenses to obtain the Certificate of Occupancy, or to cancel this contract by written notice to Seller, and any deposit shall be returned to Buyer.

GRAR
3/94

12. Risk of Loss. Risk of loss or damage to the property by fire or other casualty until transfer of title shall be assumed by the Seller. If damage to the property by fire or such other casualty occurs prior to transfer, Buyer may cancel this contract without any further liability to Seller and Buyer's deposit is to be returned. If Buyer does not cancel but elects to close, then Seller shall transfer to Buyer any insurance proceeds, or Seller's claim to insurance proceeds payable for such damage.

13. Condition of Property. Buyer agrees to purchase the property "as is" except as provided in paragraph 2, subject to reasonable use, wear, tear, and natural deterioration between now and the time of closing. However, this paragraph shall not relieve Seller from furnishing a Certificate of Occupancy as called for in paragraph 11, if applicable. Buyer shall have the right, after reasonable notice to Seller, to inspect the property within 48 hours before the time of closing.

14. Services. Seller represents that property is serviced by: _____ Public Water, _____ Public Sewers, _____ Septic System, _____ Private Well.

15. Deposit to Listing Broker. Buyer (has deposited) (will deposit upon acceptance) $ _____ in the form of a _____ with _____ (Escrow Agent) at _____ (bank), which deposit is to become part of the purchase price or returned if not accepted or if Buyer's contract thereafter fails to close for any reason not the fault of the Buyer. If Buyer fails to complete Buyer's part of this contract, Seller is allowed to retain the deposit to be applied to Seller's damages, and may also pursue other legal rights Seller has against the Buyer, including a lawsuit for any real estate brokerage commission paid by the Seller.

16. Real Estate Broker.
[ ] The parties agree that _____ brought about this purchase and sale.
[ ] It is understood and agreed by both Buyer and Seller that no broker secured this contract.

17. Life of Offer. This offer shall expire on _____ , 19 _____ , at _____ .m.

18. Responsibility of Persons Under This Contract; Assignability. If more than one person signs this contract as Buyer, each person and any party who takes over that person's legal position will be responsible for keeping the promises made by Buyer in this contract. If more than one person signs this contract as Seller, each person or any party who takes over that person's legal position will be fully responsible for keeping the promises made by Seller. However, this contract is personal to the parties and may not be assigned by either without the other's consent.

19. Entire Contract. This contract when signed by both Buyer and Seller will be the record of the complete agreement between the Buyer and Seller concerning the purchase and sale of the property. No verbal agreements or promises will be binding.

20. Notices. All notices under this contract shall be deemed delivered upon receipt. Any notices relating to this contract may be given by the attorneys for the parties.

21. Addenda. The following Addenda are incorporated into this contract:
[ ] All Parties Agreement [ ] Services [ ] Engineer's Inspection [ ] Mediation [ ] Electric Availability [ ] Utility Surcharge [ ] Lead Warning [ ] Other: _____

Dated: _____ _____ BUYER

Witness: _____ _____ BUYER

[ ] **ACCEPTANCE OF OFFER BY SELLER**   [ ] **COUNTER OFFER BY SELLER**
Seller certifies that Seller owns the property and has the power to sell the property. Seller accepts the offer and agrees to sell on the terms and conditions above set forth.
[ ] Waiver of Seller's attorney approval. This offer is not subject to Seller's attorney approval.

Reprinted by permission of the Greater Rochester Association of REALTORS®

Chapter 10

*G*etting the Best Mortgage Loan with the Least Hassle

*A*s you approach the next phase of your adventure, watch out for a malady known by the scientific name of Buyer's Remorse. Onset may be from 24 hours to two weeks after your purchase offer has been accepted. Symptoms usually develop rapidly around 2 AM, as you lie awake wondering why you ever got into this, if you can really afford the house, how you will get along without your present neighbors and whether the whole thing isn't a big mistake!

Rather than lose more sleep, call the real estate broker the next day asking if you can visit the house again, preferably when the sellers are absent. "Measuring for curtains" is a logical request; no need to alarm anyone at this point.

In nearly every case, the buyer will be pleasantly surprised during the return visit. All that hard work, research and exhausting house hunting really did pay off; this is clearly the best house in town for you.

If, as happens rarely, you are more depressed than ever after your return visit, it's time for a conference with your attorney to determine your legal position if you back out and how much money you stand to forfeit.

80. Where do I apply for a mortgage loan?

If you require a new mortgage to finance your purchase, the sales contract probably contains your promise to apply promptly at a lending institution. The real estate broker can often suggest the lender most favorable to your situation and the seller's. Perhaps this means the one that asks the fewest points this week, processes applications promptly or looks with favor on unusual older homes. Or you may be better off relying on a mortgage broker.

In some areas, the agent makes the appointment for you and even accompanies you to the application session. If you are on your own, sit down with the yellow pages open to "Mortgages" and do your own research. Ask to speak with a mortgage counselor or mortgage loan officer at the institutions you phone.

Come to the application session armed with as many facts as possible. The lender will want to know a great deal about your financial situation, all aimed at not letting you get in over your head in debt.

Factors the underwriters will consider in deciding whether to make the loan include: employment stability and other dependable income, present assets, credit history, past mortgage experience and present debts.

The lender judges two things: your ability to meet your obligations in the future and your willingness to do so, as evidenced in the past.

81. What should I take to the mortgage application?

Some of the items listed below, if not available, can be obtained later during the application process—a VA eligibility certificate, for example, or a legal description of the property. To expedite your application, though, take as much information as possible to your initial interview.

- Original purchase contract signed by all parties, which will be copied and returned to you
- Cash or check for the application fee, to cover appraisal of the property and the credit report; additional points or the origination fee if required
- Social Security numbers
- List of all income
- List of debts, credit cards, account numbers, payments, balances and addresses of out-of-town creditors
- List of two years' past employment and two years' past home addresses
- Seller's agreement to pay points (if not in the contract)
- If self-employed, two years' signed income tax returns; if on the job less than two years, copies of previous W-2s
- Expense and income statements on property presently rented out; leases signed by tenants
- Account numbers and balances on checking and savings accounts; branch addresses
- Donor's name and address for any gift letter.
- Explanation of any credit problems and copies of any bankruptcy papers
- Certificate of eligibility, if applying for a VA loan
- Legal description of the property; survey (not required for all loans)
- List of stocks and bonds and their current market value
- List of other assets
- True property tax figure on the projected purchase

- Name and phone number of the person who will give access to the lending institution's appraiser
- If paying child support or alimony; copy of the divorce decree or separation agreement; if claiming them as income, same documents, along with proof that payments are being received

82. How much should I show in assets?

You must show you have enough cash on hand for the estimated closing costs on your loan, and often for the monthly payment or two after that. Beyond this, your list of assets, particularly in a borderline situation, will influence the underwriters when they decide whether it's safe to make the loan.

You may not borrow elsewhere for the down payment (secondary financing) on some loans. A lender will be skeptical about claims that your money is under the mattress and will credit you with only a limited amount in cash—as little as $200, perhaps. The lender will also want an explanation for large sums of money that have turned up in your savings accounts within the past few months. (Maybe, the underwriters figure, you borrowed it somewhere, thus taking on too much debt.)

Bring in all details on your assets: numbers and balances on savings accounts (the lender will check with the bank to verify), a list of stocks and bonds owned, an income tax return if you anticipate a refund. Your earnest money deposit counts as an asset; the lender will verify it with the person holding the money. You may have assets you've forgotten about: cash surrender value on your life insurance policy, valuable collections, jewelry, boats and RVs, IRA, other real estate owned. List your furniture, appliances and automobiles; they might not bring much if you sold them, but they prove that you won't need to go on a buying spree right after you close on the house.

A gift letter from a relative, promising to furnish some of the funds you need for closing with no repayment required or anticipated, can sometimes be used at mortgage application.

Many lenders require the letter on their own form, and most want to verify that the relative does indeed have the funds in question.

83. What forms of income help me qualify for the payments?

Just about any kind of income, if it can be counted on in the future and can be verified, is useful. More than one borrower (husband and wife or unrelated buyers) may pool their incomes to qualify for the loan.

Ideally, two years' continuous employment in the same field indicates employment stability. Exceptions are made for recent graduates or those who have just left the armed forces. Lenders are nervous about those who jump often from one sort of job to another; employment changes that show upward movement within the same field are more acceptable.

Bonuses and overtime count toward qualification if your employer will verify them as dependable. Part-time and commission income count if they have been steady for the past year or two. Alimony and child support can be considered as income if you want to claim them, but you must be able to show that they are paid dependably and are likely to continue for the next five years or so.

Older applicants will not be asked their ages but will be asked to prove dependable Social Security and pension income if they anticipate retirement within the next few years. Disability income is counted if it is permanent.

Those on seasonal income may count it if they can prove at least a two-year history of such a cycle, and they may even be able to count unemployment insurance in qualifying.

The self-employed will be asked to furnish income tax returns for two years past and, where it's appropriate, an audited profit-and-loss statement.

Other sources of income might include dividends and interest and net rental from other properties (leases signed by your tenants may be required). If you will have rental income from the home you are buying (a duplex, for example, with the other side to be rented out), half or even all of the anticipated rent may be counted as further income.

Some special programs are specifically intended to help good applicants who might not otherwise qualify. These allow lenders to be more flexible, not requiring a two-year record of some income, for example, or taking into consideration the rent you've been managing to pay.

84. What debts count against me?

Lenders give careful consideration to present debts, or liabilities. Depending on the type of loan for which you apply, a lender will count any debt on which you must pay for more than 6, 10 or 12 months. Car loans are among the most common liabilities in this category.

Before you arrive for mortgage application, list your liabilities, including loan numbers, monthly payments, balances and time left to run. Student loans are considered obligations if payments are presently due. Child support or alimony is considered an obligation.

Watch out for credit cards. Some lenders, for certain mortgage plans, may consider that you are liable for the potential full borrowing power on each of them. That can be true even if you carry no balances.

Your assets, debts and income allow the lender to judge whether you can make the proposed mortgage payments. The final question is: are you not only able but willing to meet your obligations? That's where your credit history comes in.

It is essential to divulge information about past credit problems frankly during your interview. You should have already discussed judgments or bankruptcies with the real estate agent during your first meeting. Such problems won't necessarily prevent you from obtaining a mortgage, but if the lender's checking turns up any lies, you're in trouble.

If you've never borrowed money, don't worry. An old wives' tale says you must take out a loan and repay it to establish credit. Lenders know, though, that you've been around long enough to get into trouble if you were going to. No credit history is considered good credit.

Less-than-perfect credit may qualify you for one sort of loan and not another. VA and FHA guidelines are generally more lenient, though banks making their own portfolio loans can be flexible within certain limits. In the mid-1990s, the federal government sparked many community mortgage plans aimed at helping less-than-perfect first-time buyers qualify.

The lender may ask you for written explanations of slow payment history or any derogatory report. You will have to pay off any open judgments, even if they flow from an "I won't pay as a matter of principle" dispute.

Bankruptcy guidelines vary, depending on the type of bankruptcy and the type of loan. In general, one to two years must have elapsed since the discharge of your bankruptcy, though each case is considered separately. If your problem was due to something beyond your control, and your previous credit history was exemplary, exceptions can be made. Most important is your record of payment on any previous mortgage loan.

You'll be asked to sign a number of papers when you apply for the loan, many of them authorizing the release of verifying information from your employer, savings institution or credit bureau.

You'll also be asked for an application fee, which covers a credit report on yourself and an appraisal of the property. Sometimes other up-front fees are requested. In a time of rising interest rates, for example, you could be offered a chance to lock in the current rate for the payment of one point.

85. Then what? Do I just sit home and wait for a decision?

While the lending institution completes all the paperwork ("assembles the exhibits"), the real estate agent should keep in touch in case any hitches develop. You might check yourself from time to time to see whether things are going smoothly. Lenders have even been known to lose a whole file, so that everything has to be done again!

Within three days of your application, the lending institution must send you a good faith estimate of your closing costs and notification of your APR, the adjusted percentage rate. If you paid for the appraisal, you are entitled to receive a copy; if it isn't offered, request it in writing.

Keep the broker, or your lawyer, informed of any communication you receive from the lending institution, local government or FHA. Above all, don't go out and buy a car. This is not the time to incur additional debt or deplete your cash.

If you have questions for the seller, it's usually best to ask them through the broker, who can arrange for you to measure for curtains or show the place to your parents. Experience has proven that the transaction proceeds most efficiently when the broker and lawyers handle communication between the buyer and seller. There are exceptions, of course; sellers have been known to host a barbecue to introduce the buyers to the neighbors.

After all the exhibits have been assembled, the lender's mortgage committee reviews the underwriting decision. It may then issue either a commitment letter or a conditional commitment dependent, for example, on certain repairs to the property before closing or on your clearing up an outstanding judgment. In any event, be sure to contact the broker and your lawyer or closing agent as soon as you hear from the lender.

Once you have the commitment safely in hand, nothing remains but to find a time (within the number of days stipulated in the commitment letter) that suits everyone for transferring the property. You are ready for closing.

86. What if I need to get out of my present home before the closing?

You'll find sellers—and particularly sellers' attorneys—very reluctant to let you move in before you actually own the home. If you absolutely must in an emergency situation, be prepared for some complicated paperwork. See Chapter 22 for the seller's point of view.

In the same fashion, by the way, the seller may be unwilling to let you paint or make any improvements, even if the house is vacant, before you own the property. There's always a danger that something might go wrong and the seller would be left owning a home full of half-finished renovations.

If, on the other hand, you'd been in the house every night for a week putting in new kitchen cabinets, and your purchase fell apart at the last minute, you'd have lost your labor and materials. Anything you do to improve someone else's property becomes part of the real estate and you'd have no claim for the money or time you had spent.

Chapter 11

*W*aiting for the Keys to Your Castle

*I*n Maine, they "pass papers"; in California, they "go to escrow." It's called closing, settlement, transfer of title—the moment when the seller gets the money and you get legal ownership and the front-door keys. In few real estate matters does local custom vary so widely.

In your area, closing may be conducted by attorneys, title companies, an escrow service, the lending institution, even by real estate brokers. It may take place at the county courthouse, a bank, the title company, an attorney's office or another location. Sometimes everyone sits around a big table; sometimes buyer and seller never even meet.

87. Does it matter what day I close?

Because you will pay interest, taxes and insurance from the day you close, you'd probably prefer a closing that dovetails with your present lease so that you won't pay expenses on two different places for part or all of a month. On the other hand, you may want a few days with the new house vacant, for painting or other projects.

If you're placing a new mortgage, you'll be asked to prepay interest for the rest of the present month, to bring you up to the lender's usual "first of the month" bookkeeping. That means if you close early in the month, you'll need that much more cash. It isn't really an extra cost, of course, because you'll own the property from that day on. Still, between that and the rent you're paying, you might prefer to buy toward the end of the month.

You won't, by the way, need to make any mortgage payment on the first of the next month because mortgage interest is normally paid in arrears (the opposite of in advance). Close in June, prepay interest up to June 30th, and you won't owe any July payment because that would have been for use of the money during the month of June, and you paid that at closing. Your first payment will be due in August and will cover July's interest.

88. Do I need title insurance?

Your purchase contract provides a blueprint for the final transfer. The seller's main responsibility is to prove title, to show that you receive clear and trouble-free ownership. Depending on the mortgagee's (lender's) requirements and local custom, the seller may prove title by furnishing an abstract and lawyer's opinion, title insurance or, in some states, a Torrens certificate.

Two types of title insurance are available. One, which may be required by your lender, protects the mortgagee against loss if other parties challenge your ownership. If you need the policy for your mortgage loan, you may be asked to pay for it. The premium is a single payment, good for the whole time you own the property. For a relatively small additional fee, you can purchase at the same time an owner's policy, which protects you from loss if anyone challenges your ownership.

An abstract is a history of all transactions affecting the property, researched from the public records. Typically, the seller must furnish an up-to-date abstract and forward it to you (better yet, to your attorney) for inspection before the closing to make sure no problems exist. Where closings are handled by escrow or title companies, many of the same procedures are followed within each company.

The third method of proving title, the Torrens system, is used in some states and provides a central, permanent registration of title to the property.

89. If two of us buy together, what should concern us?

If two persons buy together, the wording of the deed determines their respective shares of ownership, their legal rights and the disposition of the property upon the death of one of them. Depending on state law, types of joint ownership include

- tenancy in common, under which each owner has the right to leave his or her share to the owner's estate;
- joint tenancy with right of survivorship, under which the survivor automatically becomes complete owner; and
- tenancy by the entirety, a special form of joint tenancy for married couples.

If the owners have unequal shares, tenancy in common is the usual form. Except with tenancy by the entirety, any owner would have the right to force a division or sale of the property (partition).

When there is more than one owner, it is important to check with an attorney to make sure the deed clearly states the desired form of ownership. If you are an unmarried cobuyer, decide what you'd want to happen if one of you died. Should the other become complete owner, or do you each want the right to leave your share to someone else in your will?

90. What is the purpose of the deed?

The deed, the bill of sale for real estate, is drawn up before closing so that it can be examined and approved. A full warranty deed contains legal guarantees: that the seller really owns the property, for example, and that no one will ever challenge your right to it. In some areas, the standard is a bargain and sale deed with covenant, or special warranty deed, which contains some guarantees but not as many as a full warranty deed. If you buy from an estate, you receive an executor's deed. A quit-claim deed completely transfers whatever ownership the grantor (person signing the deed) may have had but makes no claim of ownership in the first place.

In feudal times, when few could read or write, transfer of ownership occurred when buyer and seller walked the boundaries of the land together. Often they would take along young boys, who would serve as witnesses after buyer and seller were long gone. (One account says the boys were urged along with switches—beating the bounds—on the theory that one doesn't forget painful experiences.)

With the boundaries agreed upon, the seller would dig up a clod of earth from the land being transferred and hand it to the buyer, who seized it and, at that moment, became the new owner, "seized of the land." The legal term *seizin* still refers to the claim of ownership.

Today, in a literate society, that clod of earth is replaced by a document, the deed, whose sole purpose is to transfer ownership. The beating of the bounds is replaced by the legal description within the deed. And you become owner at the exact moment when the deed is handed to you and accepted by you—physical transfer, just as it was with that clod of earth.

91. What should I do to prepare for closing?

You'll be alerted a few days before closing as to the exact amount of money needed. Cash or a certified check is usually required; no one wants to turn over so valuable an asset on a personal check. Except where you won't attend (escrow closing), it's simplest to have a certified check or money order made out to your attorney or yourself. You can always endorse it, and matters are easier if anything goes wrong. Bring a supply of your personal checks as well.

You may be asked to bring proof that you are placing insurance on the property. Real estate in a flood-prone area may be required to carry flood insurance.

☑ Before-Closing Checklist

- ☐ Homeowner's insurance
- ☐ Flood insurance (if required)
- ☐ Water meter reading
- ☐ Electric and gas service
- ☐ Fuel supplier
- ☐ Newspaper delivery
- ☐ Telephone, cable
- ☐ Packing
- ☐ Garage sale
- ☐ Moving companies
- ☐ Change-of-address cards
- ☐ Last-minute walk-through

As closing approaches, request a last-minute walk-through of the property. If you see a window that was broken since you first inspected the house or a junked car in the backyard, don't talk directly with the seller. Instead, contact the agent and your lawyer immediately.

92. What happens at the closing?

At closing, the seller gives you a deed to the property in return for the purchase money. But you can't give the seller the cash until the lender gives you the loan. And you can't get the check for the loan until you sign the mortgage (or trust deed). And you can't sign the mortgage until you own the property.

You can see why it all must take place at once and in the right order. You are handed one paper after another, with a brief whispered explanation you're too excited to understand and the words "sign here." In some areas, buyer and seller sign all the documents ahead of time, and when everything is in order, an escrow agent, who holds all the papers, declares the transfer has taken place.

If you are assuming a mortgage, you will receive a reduction certificate, the lender's statement that the principal has been paid down to a certain amount. You should receive proof that the payments are current and that property taxes are paid up to date. A last-minute title search will reassure you that the seller did not borrow money against the property earlier that morning.

93. What if the sellers haven't done everything they promised?

It's extremely important to have last-minute problems cleared up before you hand over your check or the lender's.

Once transfer of title has taken place, many matters are *merged* into the closing—you have bought the problems along with the property. Don't rely, then, on promises that something will be taken care of "in the next few days." If it is impractical to solve the problem immediately, ask that part of the purchase price be held in escrow, to be turned over to the seller only after the matter is attended to.

In most parts of the country, it is assumed that possession will be given to you on the day of closing; in a few areas, it's customary to allow the seller a few days after that to move out.

If you agree to let the sellers remain in occupancy after closing, be sure they have plenty of financial motivation to move out as promised. Otherwise, you could find yourself stuck with a lengthy and expensive eviction. Per diem rental should be set at a high figure, with the provision that it will be deducted from that part of the purchase price held in escrow pending the sellers vacating as agreed. Sometimes the rent figure is set so it increases if they don't leave when they're supposed to.

94. What things need to be adjusted between me and the seller?

Many small items must be apportioned fairly between you and the seller. Your state will assume that the owner on the day of closing is either the seller or the buyer. Items adjusted as of the date of closing might include property taxes, interest in a mortgage being assumed or unpaid water bills.

If the tenants in the attic apartment have paid rent for the present month, part of that rent may belong to you. You should receive the security deposit they paid because someday they will ask you to return it.

When all items are listed on a balance sheet, you'll receive full credit for the earnest money deposit you placed with the real estate agent. If the lender requires a trust account, you'll be asked to place in escrow several months' property taxes and insurance costs, mortgage insurance or other items.

Various sums charged to either the buyer or seller may include recording fees (for the new deed and mortgage), attorney's fees, transfer tax (revenue stamps), notary fees, charges for document preparation, mortgage tax and closing agent's fees.

The Real Estate Settlement Procedures Act (RESPA) requires a uniform statement to be furnished to you. In addition, your attorney or the person handling the closing should furnish you with a simpler account of your expenses and credits.

95. What documents will I sign?

You'll sign two papers for the mortgage. One is the bond, or note, the personal promise to repay the loan. The other is the mortgage (or deed of trust) itself, the financial lien (claim) against the property, which gives the lender the right to foreclose if you default. Then the mortgagee gives you a check, probably the largest you'll ever see. You get to hold it just long enough to endorse it and turn it over to the seller.

The deed, which is signed only by the grantor (the seller), will be placed in your hands, then taken away to be recorded. It will probably be sent to you later. If no one is available to record the deed, go to the county recorder (usually the county clerk) and do it yourself immediately; this is of utmost importance.

You will also receive those keys and the garage door opener. You'll walk out with a mass of papers and head for the nearest glass of champagne.

Congratulations! It's been a long, complicated journey, but look how much you've learned along the way. You and your new home are going to be very happy together.

Chapter **12**

*P*icking the Right Time To Sell

*E*ach year, about half of the homes sold in the United States go to repeat buyers—mostly, to folks who have to sell their present home before buying another.

Telephone companies and van lines estimate that the average household in the United States moves once every seven years. How does this compare with your experience?

You may have no choice in the matter. A corporation may couple a promotion with a transfer across the country. Or you yourself may decide that it is worth uprooting the family for a career opportunity in another area. If yours is a military family, you must accept the fact that you may often spend only two or three years in one place.

It may be a pleasant milestone that suggests your move: an increase in income, the marriage of your last single child or retirement. Or you may be forced to sell your home because of a dramatic life change: a divorce or death in the family or a debilitating illness.

Perhaps you are unable to carry your mortgage and are facing foreclosure. In this case, immediate action is essential, as discussed at the end of this chapter.

But when your motivation is the need for more living space, you are faced with a choice.

111

96. Should I add on to my present home or buy another?

If you presently enjoy a pleasant neighborhood with favorite friends and playmates, a helpful mail carrier, a school you have confidence in or a place of worship within walking distance, you may prefer to stay put. It's much easier to improve or expand the property you have now than to start all over again in a new locality. You can retain the rose bushes you've been nurturing, the kitchen you've wallpapered and your low-interest mortgage.

It is satisfying, also, to plan precisely the home improvements you have been wanting. In adding on, you can custom-tailor two small bedrooms for the twins, put the washer and dryer where most convenient for you or build a sewing nook into the new family room.

To make the decision on a practical basis, ask yourself: Is my present house modest compared to its neighbors? If so, an additional investment in it may be prudent.

Consider a neighborhood where houses sell for approximately $175,000. Your home, though, is a bungalow worth only $130,000. It is probably safe to spend $25,000 expanding your property. Then, if you have to sell, it should be easy to find a buyer willing to pay $155,000 (or at least $150,000) to live on that particular street.

Suppose, instead, that you own a particularly impressive house on a $125,000 street, property that would be worth more than $160,000 in another part of town. As it stands, the house might bring $130,000. Beyond that price, buyers with more to spend will look in more prestigious areas.

It is obviously ill-advised to invest money in improving such property. An extra $25,000 spent on additions would increase the price by only a few thousand dollars, if that, should you have to sell.

A given street, in other words, will support only a given price range. It is economically unwise to overimprove a house for the neighborhood.

Even in the most favorable circumstances, the expansion or improvement of a house seldom raises its value by the amount of money invested. (One exception, these days, is any form of energy-saving modification.) Installation of a swimming pool, for example, may even reduce the number of potential buyers. Some will have nothing to do with a pool; others may find it pleasant but refuse to pay extra for it.

Besides the possibility of not recouping investment costs on eventual sale, there is the consideration of your present outlay. Even with the expenses of selling and buying, you may find it costs less to move to a larger home. You might even pick up, at a bargain, a house that has been generously expanded by homeowners who cannot recoup *their* costs.

If you are trying to decide whether to add on, look at nearby houses that are on the market. Open houses, usually held on weekend afternoons, allow you to visit freely without making appointments. This preparation for your sale is valuable for several reasons. For now, concentrate on how your home compares with those presently on the market.

Although asking price is not relevant to this particular decision, it is helpful to note that figure. Ask also how long the house has been on the market.

While you view these houses, make notes on the salespersons and brokers you meet, observing their techniques if you intend to sell on your own, and estimating their capabilities if you intend to list with a brokerage firm.

97. I'd like to move, but how can I, when my home is paid up and costs me almost nothing?

Such a statement may be infinitely comforting to someone who lived through the Great Depression. Many older persons feel safe in a home that they own free and clear. This emotional satisfaction is valuable.

The drawback is that it may prevent you from selling a house that no longer serves your needs, because a paid-up home is actually as expensive as any other form of housing.

If you paid $4,500 for your home before World War II, it can be difficult to understand what it means when you are told that your property may be worth $200,000. You have never seen that money, but it is yours. If you sell your home, you can add to your cost basis whatever you've spent on permanent improvements over the years and take most or all of your profit tax-free under the special provisions for homeowners aged 55 or older (outlined in Chapter 24). After selling expenses are subtracted, you might clear $185,000.

That money, invested in safe, fixed, long-term investments, will yield thousands of dollars each year. Add to that the money you presently pay for property taxes, homeowner's insurance and maintenance costs. You could probably sell your home and realize sufficient income for the rental of an apartment or other housing in a retirement or resort area.

It is important to realize that as the owner of a paid-up home, you do have an option. Each day that you remain in your home, you make a decision to keep your money in the house instead of in an income-producing investment.

This is not to say that every older homeowner should sell. Those who are comfortable should, of course, remain where they are. The gardening and small repairs that bedevil some homeowners are satisfying activities for others. The emotional stress of uprooting can be a serious consideration for the elderly.

For seniors who do want to remain at home, financial difficulties can sometimes be solved by obtaining a *reverse mortgage*. This new form of loan allows you to tap the equity in your home without having to prove any credit or income qualifications. Instead of sending in a payment every month, you receive a check from the lender. Also available are a lump-sum loan or a line of credit you can draw on.

Closing costs and interest are added to the debt, which builds up gradually against the property. No repayment is due until you sell the house or leave it permanently. The American Association of Retired Persons (AARP) has a home equity information center and a free book; for a copy, call 202-434-3525. The National Center for Home Equity Conversion publishes a list of lenders handling reverse mortgages in the states where the loans are available. The toll-free phone number is 800-247-6553.

One important consideration in favor of moving, however, is the advantage of doing so before you are forced to. If you plan to move to a warmer climate or to a one-level house or apartment eventually, you will have the benefits of better decisions if you are not under pressure. You are more likely to receive full market value for your home if you have time to spruce it up for the market, show it in favorable months of the year and consider offers at leisure.

Your choice of retirement housing also will be more satisfactory if you are free to visit resort, retirement or other desirable areas before making your decision. You can house hunt or apartment hunt at your leisure and set your own pace for moving.

98. When's the best time of year to sell?

In a perfect market, supply and demand are in balance—just as many home seekers as houses on the market—and, in an ideal situation, plentiful mortgage money is available at reasonable interest rates.

Perfection is rare in this world, though, and at any given time, your community is likely to have a sellers' market (not enough houses to satisfy demand, so that sellers can name their price) or a buyers' market (surplus housing stock available so that buyers can call the shots).

Where does your town stand at any given moment? Most real estate brokers know what sort of market prevails. To judge for yourself, look for statistics on unemployment, number of days houses remain on the market and relative sale prices.

When unemployment runs high (a large local factory closes or corporations downsize), workers leaving the area may flood the market with houses, and the few buyers remaining are able to pick and choose.

Real estate brokers should have figures for days on market (DOM) showing the number of days elapsed between the time houses go on sale and the dates of sales contracts. In a buyers' market, DOM runs several months or more.

Because many sellers have no option but to accept whatever price the buying public offers, price levels that fall near or even below those of the previous year signal a buyers' market.

If you are in no hurry to sell, you should probably try to catch a sellers' market. Except in southern resort areas, spring and early summer usually yield the highest prices. More buyers stir then because many families hope to move before the school year begins. Spring starts early in real estate; activity often heats up as early as February.

If you are selling one home and buying another, it doesn't make much difference where in the cycle you find yourself because you will have an advantage at one end or the other.

99. Should I list my house first or wait until I've found the one I want to buy?

Put your home on the market first. Almost always, and almost everywhere, it's much easier to buy than to sell. When you do find the place you want to buy, you will look much more attractive to the seller if you already have your home under contract, or at least on the market. Otherwise, you may find that the seller of the house you want won't even consider a purchase offer contingent on the sale of another house.

Often, the most favorable time to list your home is immediately after you decide to sell it. Six months before you expect to move is almost a minimum for best results. Even if satisfactory buyers for your home appear promptly, the paperwork involved in mortgage application, and the dovetailing of your needs and the buyer's, can result in problems if you are pressed for time.

If your home has not sold before you must move, you are thrust into the unenviable position of paying for two places at once. Because a vacant house seldom shows as well as one with furniture in place, your empty home may sell less readily or bring less money. And besides losing money every month, you'll be at a disadvantage when it comes to negotiating price.

Although houses have certainly been transferred in less than a week, in unusual circumstances or with no new mortgage involved, it is best to allow three to six months, when possible. You are most likely to receive the highest price for your home if you draw from the largest possible pool of buyers. An unhurried approach to your sale is the best guarantee of sufficient market exposure.

100. What should I do if there's a chance my mortgage is being foreclosed?

With many mortgages, a homeowner can technically be subject to loan foreclosure after even one late payment. But lending institutions are not eager to foreclose; most will work with a borrower who faces temporary problems.

Your first step, when trouble looms, should be to confer with your lender in person, if possible, or by phone (for starters) if your lender is located out of town. Your mortgage servicer is required by law to have a toll-free 800 phone number or to take collect calls.

Often, temporary payment schedules (interest only or FHA intervention for as long as a year) can be arranged to help deal with the problem.

When you receive written notice that foreclosure is being instituted, the worst response is to ignore it and hope the problem disappears. Once the procedure gets too far along, considerable legal fees will have been incurred. Even if you could raise the money to pay off the loan and stop the process, you would be liable for these extra costs.

If your home is sold at a foreclosure auction, the proceeds may not cover the outstanding loan, accumulated back payments and legal costs. In that case, the lender is likely to seek a deficiency judgment against you personally. The judgment—money you still must pay—could cripple your attempts to get back on your feet.

Once you have gone through foreclosure, it becomes almost impossible to place a mortgage again. From a lender's point of view, foreclosure is much worse than bankruptcy in an individual's credit history.

If real estate values have plunged in your area, the best move is to ask the lender to take back your home and forgive the debt ("deed in lieu of foreclosure"). Your attorney can explore this matter for you. Occasionally, and if you can prove you are nearly destitute, a lender agrees to accept a "short sale," cancelling the debt in return for whatever the property brings on the open market.

Depending on how far the foreclosure has progressed, your best move may be to put the house on the market. If it can be sold for a sufficient sum to clear the mortgage, prompt action is essential. Get in touch with a real estate broker, and list the house immediately, at rock-bottom price, for quick sale. If called in early enough, the broker or your lawyer might persuade the lender to hold the foreclosure process in abeyance for a few weeks. Many investors are out there looking for bargains in just such situations. You might be able to salvage your credit reputation, avoid extra legal fees and even realize leftover equity, if any.

Anyone facing foreclosure has special need for an attorney even though, in such a situation, additional legal fees are a burden.

Chapter **13**

Selling Your Home on Your Own

*I*t all depends on whom you ask, but it's likely that one or two out of every ten houses is sold without a broker's services. The National Association of REALTORS®, interviewing 4,000 homeowners, found that 81 percent bought their homes through real estate agents. At different times, lending institutions have estimated that nine out of ten mortgage applications involve brokered transactions.

101. What's a FSBO?

As soon as you advertise your own home for sale, you become what is known in real estate circles as a *FSBO* (pronounced fizzbo, "for sale by owner"). Why would you want to do it that way? You probably think it's simply to sell at full market value and pocket the commission. Often, though, FSBOs are simply intrigued by the challenge of a new task. You may look forward to mastering a new skill and hope to do it better than the professionals.

Some FSBOs tackle the job with zest and carry through the whole transaction. Those who succeed are usually sophisticated in business and financial matters. The majority of FSBOs, however, do quit and list with brokers, usually within a month, as they begin to realize the study, effort and expense involved in selling a house.

✔️ **Doing It on Your Own**

Do you have . . .

YES	NO	
☐	☐	1. Leisure time for studying, preparing, answering phone calls, showing your home?
☐	☐	2. The ability to handle disappointment or rejection?
☐	☐	3. Extra time to explore the market before you must sell?
☐	☐	4. A good lawyer who specializes in real estate?
☐	☐	5. Some sophistication in financial matters.
☐	☐	6. A realistic, nonemotional approach to your home?
☐	☐	7. Access to credit bureau information?
☐	☐	8. The ability to ask prospects face to face about their assets, income and credit rating?
☐	☐	9. Good negotiating skills?
☐	☐	10. Patience?

Passing the quiz means answering yes to at least seven of the ten questions. If you couldn't, seriously consider using a broker.

As a seller, you can eliminate the broker, but you cannot eliminate the expenses incurred and the work performed by the broker. You can provide some of the broker's services yourself; your attorney will probably do the rest. Without an agent, you must work extra closely with a lawyer. Ask in advance for advice, and never sign papers without showing them to your lawyer first.

Many people think the job of selling consists of finding someone who wants to buy your home, but that is just the tip of the iceberg. Ensuring that buyers are financially qualified, agreeing on a proper sales contract and seeing the transaction through all the paperwork down to final closing are the most important tasks.

You'll find advice for FSBOs all through the following chapters.

102. Will I hear from agents when I advertise "for sale by owner"?

Will you ever! In fact, one good way to find out which agents are on the ball and particularly interested in your area is to put out a single For Sale sign or place just one ad.

Even if you don't intend to list your home, keep a record of those agents you talk to; there's no telling where you'll be a month from now. It will help if you can recall some details about them. Did they call at a convenient time? Identify themselves promptly as agents? Sound cordial? Offer useful information? Ask permission to call later?

A FSBO's first classified ad may bring more calls from real estate agents than from prospective buyers. Instead of cutting off hopeful brokers, you can learn a great deal by chatting with them at leisure. If you feel you have sufficient sales resistance, remember that inviting a broker into your home involves no commitment on your part. You can obtain free information about the local market and educational pointers on what is involved in home selling.

103. What can I expect of an agent who comes to my home?

You should hear a classic "listing presentation," which will make some or all of the following points:

The ability to handle tension, complications and disappointment is one of the prime requisites for a good real estate agent. Every transaction is different, posing new challenges. Your agent should protect you from as much headache as possible, using expertise to anticipate, head off and absorb many of the problems in your sale. Your agent also can save some of your lawyer's valuable time. Although not allowed to practice law, brokers do perform many services and check on details that might otherwise require the attorney's effort.

Selling a home involves emotional tension. It can be difficult to free yourself of sentimental ties, view your home dispassionately and regard it as simply a piece of merchandise. Thus (your would-be agent will argue), many homeowners employ brokers for much the same reason surgeons prefer not to operate on their own relatives.

Every agent has heard stories of how "my brother-in-law sold his place himself for full price the first day," and the broker often refrains from mentioning that a house that sells within a few hours must be severely underpriced. There isn't much satisfaction in saving a 6 percent commission if you lose 10 percent of the true market value—unless, like the brother-in-law, you are blissfully unaware of what has happened.

104. Is an agent really more likely to find a buyer than I am on my own?

Some of the classic reasons for using an agent, which you will hear as soon as you start interviewing them, include the following:

Out-of-towners and relocated executives, especially when short of time, usually search a new community with a broker.

The agent deals with a pool of buyers and acts as a matchmaker. Fewer than 5 percent of buyers purchase the house they first call about. Your one classified ad is fishing with a single hook; the agent is fishing with a net. Prospects are sorted out and the appropriate ones directed to your home.

The agent screens prospects. Everyone who comes to your home should be looking for property like yours, capable of buying it and (unless you are using a discount broker) accompanied by the agent.

Buyers are even more nervous than sellers. They find agents' expertise soothing, speak to them more frankly than to homeowners and believe them more readily because they have more than one house to sell.

In the end, of course, you may find the agents' listing presentations useful simply as pointers on how to do the same things on your own!

Chapter 14

*S*electing a Good Agent

*I*f you are selling on your own, you may want to skip this chapter, although, again, you may pick up some useful information on how to do tasks usually performed by agents.

If you use an agent, among the services you can expect from a good one are the following:

- *Market analysis.* Pricing your home properly is half the job of selling. The agent will perform research, often before your initial interview, so that you have the data needed to arrive at the proper listing price.
- *Information.* At the time your home is listed, the agent will collect detailed information about the property. The material will be used not only for assisting possible buyers in choosing which homes to view, but for writing advertisements, drawing up a purchase agreement and arranging the eventual transfer of title.
- *Fix-up advice.* It can be difficult for you to view your home with an impartial eye. Being skilled in looking at houses as buyers see them, the agent can offer valuable suggestions for showing your home at its best.
- *Interim services.* If you must leave town for a vacation or move before your home is sold, you can expect the real estate agent to supervise the property, arrange for lawn care or snow removal, and check for vandalism or fire.

Neighbors seeing anything suspicious usually call the number on the For Sale sign, and the agent is available in an emergency.

- *Advertising.* Advertising costs are usually borne by the real estate firm, and they are the broker's largest single expense. The agency usually decides on the size and frequency of advertisements. You may be asked for suggestions, but you'll find that the agent is experienced in writing ads.

- *Qualifying prospects.* Unless each house hunter who visits your property is financially capable of buying it, you're just wasting everyone's time. The agent has an established technique for judging buyers and will obtain information about income, assets and credit rating within the first few minutes of conversation. The process is called *qualifying the prospect.*

- *Matchmaking.* "Buyers are liars" is a catchphrase in many real estate offices. The implication is not that buyers deliberately tell falsehoods but rather that they are motivated by many subtle influences of which they themselves are unaware.

  A family explains to an agent, quite sincerely, that they are interested only in a four-bedroom colonial in Sunny Meadows. For three months, the agent shows them every four-bedroom house that comes on the market. Finally, when yet another is listed, the agent calls to give them first chance at it, only to be told, somewhat apologetically, that they bought a house the preceding week. They had been out on a Sunday, visited an open house and fallen in love—with a three-bedroom ranch in Hidden Valley. They liked the big trees! Buyers are liars, concludes the agent.

  The agent develops skill, therefore, in reading between the lines, listening carefully and helping people find out more about their motivations than they themselves know. A large part of the work involves skillful dovetailing of buyers' needs with available homes. The agent's filing system or computer terminal will contain the names of appropriate prospects for your particular home.

- *Appointments to show.* You can expect your agent to clear appointments with you in advance, accompany all prospects and (with some exceptions) conduct the actual showing of your home. The material in Chapter 19 examines in detail the reasons, if at all possible, why you should not be present. An overzealous owner can jinx a sale. Every good broker has developed a skilled, professional technique for showing property to best advantage.

- *Open houses.* For the same reasons, your agent may recommend that you leave the property during an open house. This period, usually a weekend afternoon, is advertised as a time when the public is welcome to visit the house. Special signs invite all comers, and the agent will devote several hours to your property that day.

- *Reports on progress.* While your home is on the market, you should receive periodic calls from your agent. You will appreciate these even if the agent reports only that nothing is happening. In this case, you can expect suggestions for improving your home's appeal.

- *Negotiation of contract.* The agent's tact and diplomacy are most directly displayed in the process of bringing you into agreement with the qualified buyer who wants your property. Your own agent is legally obligated to arrange the highest possible sale price for your property (it can be worth reminding him or her of that fact), but knowledgeable in finance and law, with the experience of past transactions to call upon, the agent serves as a buffer between buyer and seller, skillfully smoothing the path to a satisfactory agreement.

- *After the contract.* With all-cash buyers scarce, the agent often helps arrange financing for your purchaser. As the mortgage market becomes more complex, expertise in finance is often the major factor in your successful sale. Unless the buyers have contracted with their own buyers' agent or employ a mortgage broker, in many areas it is customary for the agent to guide the purchaser to the most favorable lender, help with the mortgage application and supervise the complicated paperwork. During what constitutes a nervous time for all, particularly the buyer, the

agent continues to serve as liaison, also staying in touch with lawyers and the escrow or title company.
- *Transfer of title.* In the matter of final settlement, local customs differ widely. In some areas, real estate brokers run the closing session; in others, an agent is not even present.
- *After the sale.* The broker will keep all papers dealing with your sale readily available for a period of years.

105. What if I want to sell myself and an agent has "just the right buyer" on tap?

Don't pay much attention. That may simply be an attempt to get a foot in the door in hopes of talking you into listing. If, on the other hand, there really is such a prospect, you might allow the broker in and offer to pay a small commission if that specific prospect does end up buying your home. A simple written memorandum of the agreement, signed before the buyer enters, will save misunderstandings later.

106. Are there different types of agents?

Every business or profession makes subtle distinctions in rank. The difference between an associate professor and an assistant professor, for example, has considerable meaning in the academic world. So it is with real estate. Before starting your search for the best of all possible agents, you should know the significance of the different terms you will encounter.

An agent is one who has been given legal authority to act for another. A real estate agent is a limited agent, retained by you for a single purpose—to find a buyer for your property. It is worth noting that the person you hire is your agent and not the buyer's. Real estate agents are licensed in two general categories: broker and salesperson. Their licenses are issued by the state.

An entry-level license is issued to a *salesperson* (sometimes called an *agent,* as opposed to a *broker*). The salesperson is in an apprenticeship position, closely supervised by a specific broker who agrees to take legal responsibility for the salesperson's acts. Obtaining a salesperson's license usually involves study and an examination; further standards are set by the various states. It is a mistake to assume that a salesperson is necessarily an uninformed beginner. Often, an expert agent chooses to remain associated with a broker rather than to establish a separate office.

Further study, examinations and experience, and a more difficult state exam, lead to a license as a *broker*. Only a broker may collect commissions from the public. These fees are then shared with the salesperson according to a prearranged schedule; a 50/50 division is common. The salesperson provides the legwork on a transaction, and the broker furnishes supervision, backup resources and office expenses.

A REALTOR® is a broker who chooses to join a *private* organization, the National Association of REALTORS®, and usually a local association or board of REALTORS® as well. Although the state licenses brokers and salespersons, the decision to become a REALTOR® (the word is capitalized and trademarked) is personal. The REALTOR®'s salespersons may join as REALTOR-ASSO-CIATES®.

The REALTOR® subscribes to a private code of ethics, which has, in some states, been incorporated into state regulations. A local Multiple Listing Service (MLS) is usually associated with a board of REALTORS®. A smaller, similar organization, the National Association of Real Estate Brokers, designates its members as Realtists, who also subscribe to a strict code. Some agents belong to both organizations.

The trademarked word REALTOR® has become only too successful with the public. The national association, eager to keep its exclusive use of the word (like the owners of Scotch tape and Kleenex), was distressed to find in a recent survey that more than half of the people questioned thought any real estate agent was properly referred to as a REALTOR®.

107. How do I find a good agent?

Your selection should be based on

- whether the agent is currently active in your area;
- how skilled and successful the agent has been; and
- how comfortable and confident you feel with him or her.

A logical first choice is the person who sold you your home. If you were impressed with the service you received, by all means get in touch with that agent. Repeats are the most gratifying source of business, and you should receive a cordial welcome and a particularly conscientious job. If you bought your place 20 years ago, however, ask how active the agent is now and in which neighborhoods.

Referrals from friends, relatives, your lawyer or banker, co-workers or neighbors are good sources of possible agents. All are in a position to tell you what sort of service they received.

Remember, though, that the agent who did such a great job for your aunt will be of little value to you if he or she operates on the other side of the county. Agents specialize, and no one can be expert in too large a geographic area. You want someone who deals every day with buyers looking in your locality, who has on hand a complete inventory of neighboring houses on the market and who remembers prices, problems and trends from several years back.

If you are involved in a company transfer or are starting a new job in a new town, your employer may help you find an agent. Company transfer arrangements, in fact, often include extensive assistance with real estate. Appraisal of your present home, guaranteed minimum price, payment of commissions and legal fees, payment of your old mortgage for some months, house hunting and moving expenses may be offered. Your employer may even subsidize some of the interest payment on your new home if the rate is much higher than it was on your old mortgage.

Although you may not be obligated to list your home with any particular agent, those recommended by your company are probably expert and eager to do a good job so as to maintain their relationship with your firm.

Should you hire your friend Harry or cousin Delbert who is in the real estate business? The question is touchy. Consider several points:

- If Harry operates on the other side of town, or is in business only part time, he may not be the right person to sell your home.
- Doing business with a close friend or relative can be a good way to jeopardize the relationship.
- Delbert may hesitate to take money from you and end up donating valuable time instead.

If you have confidence in your friend or relative, you may want to go ahead with the listing. Should you decide not to, an explanation is in order. Feelings will be hurt if your decision is discovered when someone in the office scans the computer printout of new listings and says, "Hey, isn't this guy over on Marshall Parkway your cousin? Did you know he was listing his house?"

Instead, call your friend or relative a few days before listing and explain that you want to deal with a firm nearer home. You might also ask his opinion of the company you plan to use. The courtesy of an advance explanation will ease the situation.

108. How do I start the search for the perfect agent?

To find agents active in your neighborhood, start with the weekend classified advertising section. You should read the ads regularly in any event before listing your home in order to familiarize yourself with the current market. Brokerage offices or individual salespersons who have several nearby listings are good candidates for consideration.

Conduct a survey of For Sale signs in your area, and pay attention to Sold signs. Brokers consider the latter to be their best advertising, and with good reason.

On a weekend afternoon, drive through the neighborhood and visit open houses. You'll collect valuable information on property in competition with yours, and you can meet agents and judge their methods. The one who lounges in the living room smoking and watching television, and who waves you through the house by yourself, is a good candidate for your forget-it list.

Take notes on the agents you meet. A good agent will greet you at the door, offer a business card, ask your name and request that you sign in, furnish a fact sheet on the property, show you through in a professional manner and ask personal questions.

Although that last may not strike you as a desirable quality, it is. If you were a bona fide buyer, such questions would enable the agent to offer service. A good agent—even though the sellers' agent—will do more than simply try to sell that particular house. Open houses provide an excellent opportunity to meet prospects, and the agent may come prepared with information on similar properties and listings for the entire area, should the specific house being shown not interest a visitor.

When it becomes apparent that you are not interested in buying the house, a skilled salesperson, if not busy with other callers, will invite you to sit down and discuss real estate further. This is the time for you to explain frankly that you are trying to gather background information before putting your nearby home on the market. You won't have to guide the conversation after that!

109. Should I interview more than one agent?

Even if you are pleased with the first one you meet, it is prudent to talk with at least three, allowing them to inspect your home and make their listing presentations. Call firms active in your area, and ask them to send an agent to talk with you. You may ask for a specific salesperson whose name you have seen on signs. If you don't, either the broker in charge will assign the call or the agent on floor duty will handle the request.

An excellent way to meet prospective agents is to allow them to present themselves. Put a For Sale By Owner sign on your lawn for one day, or place one or two small classified ads. You may hear from more agents than you do buyers. Each agent who calls is obviously interested in your neighborhood, enterprising and presently free to take on listings. You won't hear from those who are inactive or currently swamped with work.

You may also find yourself flooded with house hunters on that day and even receive several written offers that evening. This means that you have mistakenly priced your home too low in the ad. Call your lawyer immediately for advice.

Your best bet is to set the price higher than you think appropriate; that teaser ad is intended simply to see which agents will contact you.

110. What type of agent will do the best job?

There is no simple answer to whether you will be better served by a man or a woman, salesperson or broker, young or old, small office or large, independent firm or one bearing a nationally franchised name. In the end, the decision comes back to your own feelings and the abilities of the salesperson you are considering. Nothing matters as much as the particular individual you choose.

A recent survey of homesellers ranked highest in importance the agent's ethics, fair treatment of all parties, knowledge of the community and mastery of financing techniques. Few considered the size of the firm important.

Your own feelings must guide you in the choice between an experienced older salesperson and an energetic younger one. The enthusiastic beginner, if properly trained and supervised, can often turn in a superior job. The broker may accompany the beginning salesperson on a listing interview. Then you can judge whether the newcomer is receiving proper supervision and how the two work together. On the other hand, you may prefer an experienced broker with a proven track record.

Do you want a part-timer or a full-timer? Many feel that only the full-time salesperson is worth trusting with a listing. The premise is that there is a greater commitment to selling real estate. On the other hand, the salesperson whose spouse is a department head at the university or a line worker with many acquaintances at the local factory often has contacts with newcomers to the area who might want your property. Although the full-time salesperson is probably a better bet, there might be good reason for you to prefer a specific part-timer. In that case, ask the broker in charge of the office whether help will be available to back up your listing agent when he or she is unavailable.

The question of whether you will be better served by an independent office versus one associated with a well known franchise is impossible to answer. So is the problem of whether to list with a large agency or a small one. Independent and small offices continue to exist, and their success makes it clear that they are selling; otherwise, they would not remain in business. Avoid those large firms that specialize in commercial properties, with perhaps only one or two salespersons in their residential departments. Their services could be too limited.

What about the broker who is also a REALTOR®? Although many good independents choose not to join the National Association of REALTORS®, the fact remains that REALTORS® subscribe to a code of ethics. Local boards have established complaint procedures and offer the opportunity for a client to submit differences to the REALTOR®'s peers. Most important, more than 80 percent of REALTORS® belong to local Multiple Listing Services, which are of great benefit to both buyers and sellers. If multiple listing is available in your area, look for a member of that system.

111. How can I judge an agent?

Some tests to apply follow:

Identification.   The well-trained, ethical agent always starts a telephone conversation or a visit to your home with "Hello, I'm Sal Salesperson of Bravo Brokers." If you suspect that some of the respondents to your one-day ad are salespeople who have not identified themselves, resolve never to do business with them.

Disclosure.   Required in writing by many states these days, and recommended everywhere, is a broker's early disclosure of agency. You can expect a good broker to discuss, early on, the various fiduciary duties that will be due to you as the seller and the fact that you will have some responsibility for your agent's actions. The status of subagents should also be discussed.

Phone Calls.   One early test of effectiveness is the agent's handling of telephone calls. This will demonstrate how easily you can reach your lister and, more importantly, how prospective buyers will be treated. Most busy agents arrange for office coverage beyond normal business hours: an answering service or answering machine. Children answering the agent's home telephone should be trained to record each call politely and accurately.

If a day or two goes by without your calls being returned, cross that agency off your list. You don't want potential buyers of your home to receive such treatment.

112. What happens when I interview an agent?

When agents arrive for listing presentations, those initial interviews in which they try to sell you on their services, they should demonstrate some preparation. They may have verified your property tax figures and lot size. This is not an invasion of privacy but the use of public information freely available to those who ask. Agents might also have a record of what you paid for the house and a comparative market analysis detailing recent sales for comparable properties. Such groundwork indicates a professional approach to the job at hand. Agents are likely also to be armed with statistics on how many listings and sales they have had in your neighborhood.

The agent who is interested in serving you must determine your needs. Questions such as "When do you need to move?" and "Where are you planning to go?" are not impertinent. Rather, they demonstrate the kind of information gathering that marks a skilled agent. You want someone who can ask similar questions of prospective buyers.

While you interview agents, stay alert for the one who is familiar with special programs at the local grade school, serves on the Scout committee and knows why the fast-food operation was turned down for the spot on Main Street. Local expertise is vital to good service and usually indicates an agent who is genuinely interested in real estate.

Ask whether the broker takes phone calls at home and how the office phone is covered after business hours. If the broker has a beeper or car phone, that may help down the line at a point where quick contact is necessary.

If the salesperson does not volunteer information on recent dealings, ask for it. Ask also about training and courses of study

in real estate. You may eventually decide to go with a person-
able newcomer, but you should know how long your agent has
been in the business and what kind of success has been
achieved.

113. How important is the agent's price recommendation?

A knowledgeable homeowner has been known to mention a
ridiculously high asking price just to test the reactions of
potential listers. The agent is in a delicate position. He or she is
torn at this point. Sounding pessimistic about securing that
price, the agent runs the risk of losing your listing. But a
professional salesperson knows that an overpriced listing receives little attention, wasting time and advertising dollars.

A good agent will try, as tactfully as possible, to talk you out
of an unreasonably high price. While hesitating to criticize your
home, an agent may be inclined to make suggestions for en-
hancing its appeal. Beware of the agent who agrees readily to
your ambitious price and promises a sale within a week. Houses
are not supposed to sell that quickly.

You do not, on the other hand, want to list with a person
who demonstrates no enthusiasm for your property. An agent
should not play on your fears or denigrate your home in an
attempt to pick it up at a bargain. Of course, you may encounter
someone who is by nature reserved and unenthusiastic. Unless
that suits your own outlook, you are better off with an agent
who gets reasonably excited about your home.

114. What educational background can I expect an agent to have?

The beginning salesperson may have studied only the material required by the state for licensing. As time goes on, however, top agents are likely to attend seminars, real estate conventions, training sessions and college courses in appraisal, finance or construction.

Designations, awarded by brokers' organizations, are usually earned after study and examinations and require certain levels of experience. Among the more common are the GRI (Graduate of the REALTORS® Institute), held by about 10 percent of REALTORS®, and the CRS (Certified Residential Specialist), for which about 3 percent of REALTORS® have qualified. While no guarantee of expertise, the designations do show that you've met somebody who has invested time and effort in the business and is experienced.

Multiple listing is a help with your sale, and if no Multiple Listing Service is available in your area, ask whether the agent cooperates with other offices that might want to show or sell your home. Such arrangements must be made by the broker, not by the individual salesperson with whom you speak; office policy is well established in this matter. You should work with an office that will cooperate fully with others.

If your home is eventually sold by a cooperating broker from another company, you are not normally responsible for any extra commission. Discuss this point with your agent, just to make sure. Ask what share of the commission will be offered to the subagent from another firm who might produce your buyer. In some communities, a 50/50 split is common, but the listing brokerage can set its own figure. If not enough is promised to a cooperating firm, other agents in a Multiple Listing Service may not be motivated to work on your property, thus cutting down on the number of potential buyers.

115. Should I agree to cooperate with buyers' brokers?

Certainly. Whatever widens the pool of possible buyers operates to your advantage. Ask also about your listing company's policy on buyer brokerage. If another agent is paid by the buyers to represent them, will your company cooperate in showing the property and negotiating a sales contract? Will your agency consider appropriate adjustments to commission?

Buyers' brokers are a relatively new group, and some firms may not be accustomed to working with them. Old-time brokers should not feel threatened by this new arrangement, though, and neither should you. If you refuse to deal with buyers' brokers, you eliminate a valuable pool of prospects.

Ask what will happen if the firm with which you list also serves as broker for a buyer who wants your home. There are various ways to meet the problem of potential conflict of interest.

Discuss also whether, in the event your home is sold by a buyer's broker, you would allow the buyer's agent to share in the commission. Although that may seem like a peculiar arrangement, it often ends up that way, simply because most buyers don't have much extra cash left. It does not entail any extra charge to you. Cross off the list immediately any agent who tells you that commissions are set by law or by the local board of REALTORS®. This just isn't so. Commission rates are completely negotiable between you and the agent, although a salesperson requires the broker's permission to change the office's customary rate. Guidelines in the matter of commission rates are discussed in Chapter 16.

116. What else should I look for in an agent?

Most agents, during an interview, will offer to leave a sample listing contract with you; if they don't, ask for it. You can then study the document at your leisure.

An explanation of the types of listing contracts open to you can be found in Chapter 16. One arrangement, however, should trigger a red light. If an agent proposes to guarantee you a certain sum from your sale, in return for the chance to keep anything over that amount, you have been offered a net listing. This arrangement is open to so much abuse that it is illegal in about half of the states. You can view with suspicion any practitioner who suggests it.

At first, the net listing may sound seductive; you receive the agreed-upon sum from the sale of the property, and the agent assumes all the risk that the sale price is not higher. But any number of complications may arise. The agent might be tempted to block an otherwise attractive offer; although the law requires that you, as the client, must come first, the agent's own interests are paramount.

One good way to judge a broker is to see whether you receive a follow-up call a few days after the listing presentation. You'd want an agent who routinely checked back with prospective buyers, wouldn't you?

117. What is a guaranteed sale?

In some circumstances, you need to know that you can count on a certain minimum sum by a given date. Some offices can offer you a guaranteed sale. In essence, it is a promise to buy your property at a discounted price if it has not been sold by your deadline. Any guarantee should be in writing, and you need assurance that, meanwhile, the office intends to market the property aggressively and to try for a higher price.

The broker is justified in offering a price well below market value. Remember that the broker buys your home at wholesale. It is worth much more to the homebuyer who intends to live in it. Some of the broker's costs, if he or she does buy your home and then resells it, include an average of three months' taxes, insurance, utilities and lost interest on the investment while the house is vacant. Legal fees for buying and again for selling, maintenance costs, emergency costs and points (explained in Chapter 21) must all be considered. The broker will also include the lost commission on the eventual buyer, who might otherwise have been sold another home.

If a guaranteed sale is contemplated, the broker should explain these factors to you and furnish an estimate of true market value. The broker should counsel you to price your home attractively in hopes of selling it at retail within your time limit.

118. Do I need a lawyer?

Yes. The law does not require you to have legal representation to sell a house. In many areas, local custom does not expect it either. Nevertheless, you are well advised to have your own lawyer from the beginning of the transaction, no matter where your home is located.

In many areas, sellers routinely expect to employ attorneys to help prove that they can furnish marketable title to the property, to draw up the deed that transfers the real estate, to field problems and to represent the sellers at closing. In other parts of the country, transfer may be effected by title companies or special escrow companies, which perform many of the same tasks as attorneys. Even in those areas, though, prudent homeowners retain their own lawyers. You can explain to your attorney that you may require limited services to supplement those for which you will pay a title company.

It is always appropriate to discuss fees in advance. A law firm may charge a percentage of the sales price of your home or may bill you by the hour for services actually performed. Extra charges are acceptable if an unforeseen snag arises, but a lawyer should be able to estimate the cost of your transaction.

Remember that lawyers specialize, and that you want one who is active in real estate. Start your search with a lawyer who has performed other services for you; consider the one who represented you when you bought your home.

Beyond that, you can request a list of lawyers from your real estate broker. Your agent knows which attorneys are active in real estate work. You need not fear conflict of interest; the lawyer is well aware of fiduciary duty to you as a client.

Lending institutions can be a source of information in this matter. Call a local savings and loan office and ask about law firms that handle the S&L's own real estate transactions. This is a particularly good way to find the best attorney in a new town.

The law does not forbid an attorney's representing both you and the buyer, although ethics discourage the practice. It may occur in small towns where there is not much legal talent to choose from. The lawyer must withdraw, however, if a conflict arises.

When you select your lawyer, preferably before starting to market your home, be frank about any problems, either with the property or in your own situation. Unpaid judgments, an impending divorce, an electric system that you know violates code—all represent exactly the sort of complications for which you want legal assistance. Attorneys spend much of their time heading off trouble. If you employ one and conceal your problems, it's like seeing a physician and concealing your symptoms.

Chapter 15

*U*nderstanding Your Agent's Many Responsibilities

*I*t is important that you understand the fiduciary duties owed you by your agent. Those legal obligations are discussed in detail from the buyer's point of view in Chapter 2, which you may want to look over. The agent must put your interests above anyone else's and owes you obedience (to lawful instructions), confidentiality (except about hidden defects in the property), notice (any information that would help your negotiating position) and accounting of any funds held during your transaction. Your agent owes buyers only honest treatment.

It is important to remember that any agent officially retained as the buyer's broker does not owe you any duty of confidentiality. You might not want to tell the buyer's broker anything you wouldn't want the buyer to hear, as, for example, that you would accept less for the property than the listed price.

Primary to the fiduciary relationship is a requirement that your broker put your interests above everyone else's, including the broker's own. The broker owes you complete loyalty; anything short of that is considered a breach of duty. One of your agent's primary duties is to obtain the highest possible price for your property.

Buyers are not your broker's clients. The law requires that a seller's broker be trustworthy in dealing with buyers, and a good broker will know the buyers well and identify their needs. Nevertheless, legally speaking, buyers are merely customers unless they have specifically hired their own brokers. When push comes to shove, your broker's complete loyalty is due to you, the client.

Most important, your broker must inform you of any facts, figures or trends that may help your negotiating position. If the buyer tells your agent, "We'll pay more if we have to," your broker is duty-bound to pass that information on to you.

Your agent is not permitted to screen or block offers but must present any written offer to you immediately.

The broker may not divulge confidential information that is not in your best interest. The broker may not suggest an offering price less than your listed figure without your authorization or reveal the figure at which you have confided that you might sell.

The broker is required to maintain a separate escrow account in which the buyer's deposits are kept until time of transfer. You have the right to know the amount and form of any deposits. In the event of dispute, the broker should not return deposits to the buyer without your authorization.

The broker also owes you continuous bona fide efforts to obtain a satisfactory purchaser for your home. This duty implies advertising, which is usually paid for by the broker, and showing your property. Unless your property is in a hard-to-find or distant location, you can reasonably expect a good agent to show every prospect through personally. At times, another salesperson from the same office may take over.

You will want to hear how often your home is being shown. (Cooperating brokers from other offices who enter while you are away should leave identifying cards on your kitchen counter.) You want to know what potential buyers say about your property and what other brokers say.

You are entitled to these reports even if only to learn that nothing is happening. A top agent will have suggestions to make in that case—ways to enhance your home's appeal. You may hear a tactful plea that you not participate in showings. Where price is the problem, the agent may suggest meeting with you to discuss steps that may be taken. If price is not the issue, you may eventually want to offer a bonus of a few hundred dollars to the salesperson who sells you home.

If you do not receive regular reports of progress, never hesitate to call and ask. Agents who furnish a home phone number are used to receiving calls in the evenings and on weekends and will not resent them.

Keep yourself available. If you leave town on a vacation, alert your agent to keep an eye on the house. Make sure the property can be shown, and leave your temporary phone number with the agency. An offer can be communicated by telephone and fax when quick action is needed.

119. Can I dismiss an unsatisfactory agent?

Probably. Can you recover for damages suffered because of incompetence or breach of fiduciary duties? Possibly. For advice on either situation, talk with your lawyer.

Long before affairs reach such a state, however, you can take a number of steps to lodge your complaints. The first and simplest step is to speak with the agent directly, communicating your dissatisfaction as openly as possible.

If this brings no results, talk with the managing broker in the office. Don't be afraid to make a pest of yourself. If telephone calls don't bring satisfaction, write a letter (keeping it as brief as possible) indicating the next steps you intend to take. Most brokers are highly sensitive to sellers' complaints and will intervene immediately to straighten things out.

Next, before going beyond the immediate office, it may be wise to speak with your attorney. If you want to cancel the listing, in many cases you have only to ask. Depending on the terms of your listing contract, the type of agency granted and state law, you may be able to cancel at will or you may be able to cancel with repayment to the broker for time and money expended. If you are told that the office does not cancel listings, a call from your attorney may break the deadlock. Multiple Listing Services may look with disfavor on a broker who picks up a canceled listing and resubmits it, so check the procedure if you plan to transfer to another MLS office.

If you want to blow the whistle on a broker, a number of options are available. The local chamber of commerce and better business bureau have no jurisdiction over agents. Neither does the action line or help column of the local newspaper or television station. But a threat that you will complain to them may touch a nerve for the broker because public opinion and reputation are vital to the real estate brokerage business.

More serious is a complaint to the local board of REALTORS®, if your broker is a member. The real estate industry is eager to retain as much self-regulation as possible and has set up procedures for enforcing its code of ethics. Your broker's actions will come under serious scrutiny by his or her peers, and your problem should receive prompt attention.

Finally, you can report any serious violation to the state licensing commission. This is strong medicine, for this body, in addition to lesser punishments, can deprive brokers of their licenses, putting them out of business. The mere mention of a plan to contact the licensing commission usually brings prompt response from recalcitrant agents.

When a serious offense has damaged you materially, your attorney can advise whether a lawsuit is in order. If you should win a suit against a broker who cannot be reached for collection of damages, you may be able to tap your state's recovery fund (if available), to which brokers contribute regularly.

Where a relatively small amount of money is involved, you can represent yourself in small claims court at little expense. If you plan to do so, however, discuss the case with an attorney beforehand for advice on how to proceed.

Chapter *16*

*N*avigating Your Listing Contract

*M*ost of this chapter deals with the process of formally listing your home for sale through a broker. Read it even if you are selling on your own because without an agent, you will list the house with yourself, and your first task will be careful gathering of the information detailed in the second half of the chapter.

120. What obligation do I have if I invite agents to my home?

Agents who come to your home to make listing presentations have the task of convincing you that they are the right persons to handle your property. These initial interviews will cost you nothing, and you will not be obligated in any way. Even if you like the first agent who calls, it can be educational to talk with several others before making your decision. You are not obligated until you sign a listing contract.

The listing is an employment contract under which you agree to pay a commission to the broker for securing a purchaser who is ready, willing and able to pay the price and comply with the terms that you have specified. Strictly speaking, this contract might be enforceable by the broker even if you were not the owner of the property and even if the transaction were never completed. In theory, the broker's function is fulfilled when he or she finds a buyer who satisfies the requirements you have specified. In practice, the listing contract often contains provisions further regulating the payment of commission to protect both you and the broker. You may want your lawyer to review the contract before you sign it.

121. What types of listing contracts are possible?

Oral. In approximately half the states, a listing need not be in writing to be enforceable. Although the statute of frauds everywhere requires that real estate contracts be in writing, a promise to pay a licensed broker a commission for aid in selling real property can be an exception. Even accepting the services of a broker, without any promise to pay commission, has sometimes been held by the courts as an implied contract of employment.

Net. In a net listing, the sellers agree to a certain figure as their share of the selling price. Monies beyond that sum remain with the broker as commission. As previously pointed out, this type of listing is seldom in your best interest and is illegal in many states.

Open. On a country road, you may come across an isolated house with three or four For Sale signs in its yard, each bearing the telephone number of a different agency. This house is being marketed through open listings. The owners have promised a number of agents that they will pay a commission to the firm that produces a satisfactory sale. If the owners should sell on their own, no commission would be payable to anyone.

The open listing is often used in rural areas that lack multiple-listing arrangements, so that you may use the services of several agents in nearby towns. Its simplicity is attractive, and it appears to be in your interest. Any particular agent, however, may lack the incentive to invest heavily in advertising or to spend time marketing your property. If a competing office effects the sale, the hours and money spent are not reimbursed in any way. It can be difficult to obtain maximum effort from those with whom you have open listings.

Exclusive.   These listings fall into two categories—exclusive agency and exclusive right to sell. With the first, you retain the right to sell the property on your own, without owing a commission. This constitutes the major difference between them.

Exclusive agency promises that the listing office will be your only agent. If anyone is to receive a commission, a member of that firm will. You retain the right, however, to sell the property yourself without paying a commission. In effect, you compete with your own agent.

Exclusive right to sell is a promise of commission if the property is sold by anyone during the listing period. Even if you sell it yourself, you still owe a commission. With the protection this affords, a listing office is theoretically motivated to go all out on the assignment.

In a Multiple Listing Service (MLS), your agent shares the listing with a number of other brokers. If one of these finds the buyer, your original firm will receive a share of the commission, usually around 50 percent, depending on local custom. You will not be liable for any extra payment.

A listing that is thus shared might, in theory, be any of the types mentioned, but exclusive right to sell is the type most often required by a Multiple Listing Service. It is difficult to understand that you can sign an exclusive right to sell with hundreds of different offices; somehow, that doesn't seem very exclusive. Each one becomes your subagent, however, unless you specifically state that you don't want that relationship. Some sellers fear they could be held liable for misrepresentations or human rights violations that might be made by cooperating brokers who serve as their subagents.

Members of Multiple Listing Services can also, if desired, accept listings that will be truly exclusive to one firm. Although the MLS is usually the most efficient way to market your property, you might prefer to deal with a single office. If you desire a silent sale (one that is not publicized), multiple listing is not for you because the system widely disseminates information about your home.

122. Can I try negotiating the commission rate?

You certainly can—if the listing broker agrees to negotiate.

Each brokerage firm sets its own rate schedule. Rates in a given community may tend to cluster around 6 percent or 7 percent. Some types of real estate commonly listed at higher rates are vacant land, farms, resort property, inexpensive parcels and property that is difficult to market.

In an area of expensive homes, on the other hand, you may be able to negotiate a lower fee than a firm's usual rate. Before making any such arrangement, however, a number of factors must be considered. Will the contract be placed in a Multiple Listing Service, where the lower commission rate won't motivate cooperating brokers? Does the broker who operates below usual rates have a sufficient budget for advertising?

Sellers have been known to make separate agreements with members of a Multiple Listing Service in this manner: "If you have to share the commission with another office, I'll pay 6 percent. But if you sell it yourselves and receive the whole commission, let's settle for 5 percent." This sort of proposition is more attractive to brokers when it is linked to an expensive, sensibly priced house.

You may be approached by a discount broker, who offers limited, unbundled services. Find out exactly what is involved and which tasks you may be asked to perform for yourself. Most

LISTING BROKER'S COPY

GREATER ROCHESTER ASSOCIATION OF REALTORS®, INC.
EXCLUSIVE RIGHT TO SELL CONTRACT

THIS FORM IS FOR USE BY MEMBERS OF THE GREATER ROCHESTER ASSOCIATION OF REALTORS®, INC. ONLY FOR THE PLACING OF PROPERTY LISTINGS IN ITS MULTIPLE LISTING SERVICE.

REALTOR® EXCLUSIVE RIGHT TO SELL, EXCHANGE OR LEASE CONTRACT. COMMISSIONS OR FEES FOR REAL ESTATE SERVICES TO BE PROVIDED HEREUNDER ARE NEGOTIABLE BETWEEN REALTOR® AND OWNER. IT IS UNDERSTOOD THAT THE GREATER ROCHESTER ASSOCIATION OF REALTORS®, INC. (including its MLS) IS NOT A PARTY TO THIS LISTING AGREEMENT.

1. **OWNERSHIP OF PROPERTY AND POWER TO SIGN CONTRACT.** I am the Owner(s) of the property located at _____ (the Property). I have complete legal authority to sell, exchange or lease the Property. I have not entered into any other agreement which would affect the sale, exchange, lease, or transfer of the Property; except as follows: (name or specify agreement.)

2. **EXCLUSIVE RIGHT TO SELL, EXCHANGE OR LEASE.** (Check and complete either (a) or (b)).

(a) _____ I hereby hire _____ (REALTOR®), to sell or exchange the Property and I hereby grant to REALTOR® the Exclusive Right to Sell the Property for the price of $ _____ or any other price that I later agree to, and upon such terms and conditions as I may agree to or to exchange the Property upon such terms and conditions as I may agree to.

(b) _____ I hereby hire _____ (REALTOR®) to lease the Property and I hereby grant to REALTOR® the Exclusive Right To Lease the Property for a rent of _____ per _____ or any other rent that I may later agree to, and upon such terms and conditions as I may agree to.

3. **MULTIPLE LISTING SERVICE.** I authorize REALTOR® to submit the information contained in this listing agreement and the applicable Greater Rochester Association of REALTORS®, Inc. Profile Sheet relating to the Property to the Multiple Listing Service of the Greater Rochester Association of REALTORS®, Inc. (MLS). REALTOR® will submit such information to the MLS through REALTOR®'s MLS terminal (or by first class mail or telecopy if REALTOR® does not have a MLS terminal) **within 48 hours** of my signing this Contract, excluding Saturdays, Sundays and holidays. REALTOR® shall retain this listing agreement and the Profile Sheet for at least six years.

4. **PAYMENT TO REALTOR®.** (Check and complete either (a) or (b), or both).

(a) _____ I will pay REALTOR® a commission of _____ % of the sale price of the Property, as set forth in the purchase and sale contract that I sign, or $ _____ if the Property is exchanged.

(b) _____ I will pay REALTOR® a commission of _____ % of the gross rent for the Property as set forth in the lease contract that I sign, or such other compensation arrangement as is agreed upon in writing, a copy of which is attached.

5. **AUTHORIZATION REGARDING OTHER BROKERS.** I authorize REALTOR® to cooperate with other brokers, including brokers who represent buyers (with the understanding that such "buyers' brokers" will be representing only the interests of the prospective buyers), to appoint subagents, and to divide with other licensed brokers such compensation in any manner acceptable to REALTOR®, such other brokers and me. I understand and agree that if the commission provided for in Paragraph 4 is divided, it will be divided as follows: _____

6. **PAYMENT OF COMMISSION.** I agree to pay to REALTOR® the commission set forth in Paragraph 4 on the "closing date" specified in the purchase and sale contract or when I sign a written agreement to exchange the Property or when I sign a lease for the Property. I will pay this commission to REALTOR® whether I, REALTOR®, or anyone else sells, exchanges or leases the Property during the life of this Contract. REALTOR® has earned the commission when I am provided with a written purchase offer which meets the price and other conditions I have set or when the purchase and sale contract becomes a binding legal commitment on the buyer, or when I sign a written agreement to exchange the Property, or when I sign a lease for the Property. At the closing of the sale of the Property, my representative (such as my attorney) is authorized to pay to REALTOR® the commission agreed to in Paragraph 4 from the proceeds of the sale of the Property.

7. **DUTIES OF REALTOR® AND OWNER.** REALTOR® will bring all offers to purchase, exchange or lease the Property to me. I agree to refer all inquiries about the Property to REALTOR®. I agree to cooperate with REALTOR® in showing the Property to possible buyers or renters at any reasonable hour. I agree that REALTOR® may photograph the Property listed for sale, exchange or lease.

Check One

8. SUBMISSION OF OFFERS TO PURCHASE.
I agree that any offers to purchase, exchange or lease the Property shall be
submitted through: _____ the listing broker _____ the selling broker

9. FOR SALE, FOR RENT SIGN. Authorization to install a "or sale" or "for
rent" sign placed on the Property: _____ Yes   _____ No

10. LOCKBOX. Authorization of the use of a lockbox. I understand that
neither REALTOR®, any cooperating broker, the Greater Rochester Association
of REALTORS®, Inc. nor its MLS shall be responsible for any theft, loss or
damage attributed to the use of a lockbox.   _____ Yes   _____ No

11. PROPERTY CONDITION DISCLOSURE. I have completed and
delivered to REALTOR® a Real Estate Transfer Property Condition Disclosure
Statement concerning the condition of the Property: _____ Yes   _____ No

**12. LIFE OF CONTRACT; SALE, EXCHANGE OR LEASE OF PROPERTY AFTER CONTRACT ENDS TO A PERSON WHO WAS SHOWN
THE PROPERTY DURING THE LIFE OF CONTRACT.** This Contract will last until midnight on _____, 19_____. However,
if I sell, exchange or lease the Property within _____ days after this Contract ends (the "Effective Period") to a person who was shown
the Property by Owner(s), REALTOR®, or anyone else during the life of this Contract, I will pay REALTOR® the same commission agreed
to in Paragraph 4 of this Contract. I will not owe any commission to REALTOR® if such sale, exchange or lease occurs during the life of
a Greater Rochester Association of REALTORS®, Inc. MLS Contract I enter into after this Contract ends but before the expiration of the Effective
Period.

13. PUBLICATION OF PROPERTY DATA. I agree that REALTOR® may provide MLS with information, including the selling price, about
the Property upon final sale of the Property. I further agree that REALTOR® may provide MLS with information, other than price, prior to final
sale of the Property.

14. INFORMATION ABOUT PROPERTY. All information about the Property I have given REALTOR® is accurate and complete, and
REALTOR® assumes no responsibility to me or anyone else for the accuracy of such information. I authorize REALTOR® to obtain other information
about the Property if REALTOR® wants to do so. REALTOR® will use sources of information REALTOR® believes to be reliable, but is not
responsible to me nor for the accuracy of the information REALTOR® obtains. I authorize REALTOR® to disclose to prospective purchasers and
any other persons including other brokers any information about the Property REALTOR® obtains from me or any other source. I understand
that New York law requires me to give certain information about heating and insulation to prospective purchasers if they ask for it in writing
before a purchase contract is signed.

15. NON-DISCRIMINATION. I understand that the listing and sale, exchange or lease of the Property must be in full compliance with local,
state and federal fair housing laws against discrimination on the basis of race, creed, color, religion, national origin, sex, familial status, age
or disabilities.

16. RESPONSIBILITY OF OWNER(S) UNDER THIS CONTRACT. All Owners must sign this Contract. If more than one person signs this
Contract as Owner, each person is fully responsible for keeping the promises made by the Owner.

17. RENEWAL AND MODIFICATION OF CONTRACT. I may extend the life of this Contract by signing a renewal agreement. If I renew
this Contract, REALTOR® will notify MLS of the renewal. All charges or modifications of the provisions of this Contract must be made in writing,
signed by Owner(s) and REALTOR®.

18. LIST OF BROKERS. I hereby certify that REALTOR® has provided me with a list of names and addresses of all MLS member companies.

19. OWNER'S LIABILITY FOR CONTRACT TERMINATION. In the event this Contract is terminated prior to the time specified in Paragraph
12 for any reason other than REALTOR®'s fault, I will be liable for and agree to pay all damages and expenses incurred by REALTOR®,
including without limitation costs for advertising the Property.

20. ATTORNEY'S FEES. In any action, proceeding or arbitration arising out of this Contract, the prevailing party shall be entitled to reasonable
attorney's fees and costs.

21. NOTICE TO HOMEOWNERS. The Secretary of State, State of New York, requires that the following explanation be given to homeowners
and acknowledged by them in the listing of property:

EXPLANATION:

An "exclusive right to sell" listing means that if you, the owner of the property, find a buyer for your house, or if another broker finds a buyer, you must pay the agreed commission to the present broker.

An "exclusive agency" listing means that if you, the owner of the property find a buyer, you will not have to pay a commission to the broker. However, if another broker finds a buyer, you will owe a commission to both the selling broker and your present broker.

Owner(s) understands that this Contract grants REALTOR® the exclusive right to sell the Property.

Acknowledgement of Explanation:

_____   _____
OWNER(S) SIGNATURE   OWNER(S) SIGNATURE   Date: _____

In consideration of the above, I accept this Contract and agree to its terms and conditions.

_____   _____
OWNER(S) SIGNATURE   OWNER(S) SIGNATURE

_____   _____
Print Owner(s) Name   Print Owner(s) Name   Date: _____

In consideration of the above, REALTOR® agrees to use best efforts to find a purchaser.

_____   _____
Print Name of REALTOR®   Print Name of Broker or Salesperson

                                  _____
                                  Signature   9/91

REALTOR

Reprinted by permission of the Greater Rochester Association of REALTORS®

often, the discount broker saves time by sending buyers to your home instead of accompanying them. If you use a discount broker, make sure your home will be entered in the Multiple Listing Service with enough commission offered to the traditional firm that may produce a buyer.

123. How long should the listing last?

One month is too short a period for the agent's protection; some of the marketing techniques will just be getting under way. One year, on the other hand, is unfair to you unless you are selling rural property. In general, real estate that is correctly priced should sell within three months, except in depressed markets. The agent may ask for a six-month period instead or even write in a six-month expiration date without asking your permission. Remember that the length of time is at your discretion and that you want the contract to contain an expiration date with no automatic renewal. Check these points before you sign the listing contract.

Your agent will probably use a standard listing form, which may include a carryover stipulation. This states that if the property is sold after the listing has expired to someone who first saw it while the listing was in force, a commission will be due. The provision protects the agent from exerting effort and investing money in your property while you wait out the listing, make a private deal with one of the firm's customers and cut the agent out of a commission. The number of days this provision remains in effect can vary; 60 days after expiration of the listing is probably long enough to protect the agent.

If you are using a Multiple Listing Service, you may have specific reasons for preferring not to talk with other agents: a sick person in the house, perhaps, or a general dislike of telephone conversations. You may stipulate that all appointments be made through your listing office or that your own agent accompany everyone, even other brokers with their customers. Such restrictions, however, limit your chances of selling. If your own agent is not available when another broker is ready to show the property, your home will be ignored.

In some localities, you may be asked to furnish a certificate of occupancy for certain properties, particularly multiple dwellings. Your broker can explain what is involved. If this certificate is required, the listing should state clearly whether you agree to furnish it.

Pets on the premises are sometimes mentioned in the comments accompanying a multiple listing so that other offices are aware of the large dog in the basement or the cats shut up in the garage. Special showing instructions can also be included: please turn down heat; back door must be slammed; leave lights on over those funny plants in the cellar.

124. What financing information is listed?

Financing possibilities may be detailed at the time of listing. You will be asked to set the price you want, a topic that deserves a chapter all its own (see Chapter 17), and the terms on which you will sell. It is simplest to say "all cash," for you can always accept different terms later. If you are willing to take back financing (hold the mortgage yourself), or if you have an assumable mortgage, these selling points should be broadcast at the outset.

Try to learn about the mortgage situation in your area and on your specific house. Your agent may need your mortgage number, and perhaps your specific authorization, to obtain information on your present loan or loans.

If you are selling on your own, investigate for yourself. Talk with your mortgage holder to determine not only the present balance on the loan, but whether it will be of any value to the next owner of your home. Some old Federal Housing Administration (FHA) and Department of Veterans Affairs (VA) loans may be taken over (assumed) exactly as they stand by any buyer.

Newer VA and FHA mortgages and some conventional loans, particularly adjustable-rate mortgages, might be "assumable with lender's approval." This means the buyer must meet bank standards and possibly pay a higher interest rate than you do. Find out whether your present mortgage is assumable in any fashion and what closing costs (usually a small amount) would be involved.

Ascertain at this point whether you will be subject to a prepayment penalty if you pay off your current loan in full before the end of the term.

Find out whether new FHA and VA loans are available in your area and whether loan limits would cover your home. If so, they may be useful to many potential buyers.

Your agent should discuss at the time of listing whether you are likely to be asked for specific repairs by a buyer's prospective lender. These potential costs should be considered from the start. A further explanation of repairs can be found in Chapter 17.

If you are selling on your own, it is essential to estimate beforehand how much income a buyer might need to qualify for a mortgage loan on your property. Of course, you can't guess how much a prospective buyer might have for down payment or how many other debts might cut the available loan amount. You should, however, study the material on qualifying ratios in Chapter 21 so that you have a rule of thumb to use when you size up prospects.

125. What else should I discuss at listing?

Many things beyond those noted in the contract.

For example, may a For Sale sign be placed on your property? You must give permission. Do so by all means. The sign is one of the best advertisements your home can have. It will give the firm's name and telephone number and may also state "by appointment only" so that you will not be bothered by unexpected callers. A sign should not be placed, however, if the neighborhood is overloaded with property for sale, if local regulations forbid signs or if you have an overriding need for privacy regarding your sale.

Will the broker hold open houses? The proper time to discuss this possibility is at listing. Sellers often don't realize that few sales result from open houses, but if you want the broker to schedule them, talk about it now.

Discuss also hours for showing the proeprty. It is wise to place as few restrictions as possible. You may not want your home shown on certain days of the week or while an invalid or a shift worker sleeps. You may prefer that no one visit during the children's naps or when you eat dinner. Some sellers request 24 hours' notice before a showing.

Every one of these restrictions, however, limits your chances of finding the right buyer. Out-of-towners in particular are often under rigid time limitations. They may need to find a house in one day, and those that can be viewed promptly stand the best chance of being chosen.

What about a key? Do not hesitate to leave one with your lister's office for use when you are not at home. The lister will notify other brokers that the key is available and keep careful track of who borrows it. If you dislike giving out the key permanently, do so at least when you go on vacation or leave town for the weekend; otherwise, your home is effectively off the market for those periods.

In some areas, it is common to use lockboxes for properties whose owners are often absent. The lockbox is a gadget attached to your door, with your door key inside it. The box can be opened by cooperating brokers; it is then a simple matter to access your home when you are away. If potential buyers spot the sign and want to see your house, an agent can show it without an appointment.

Although the lockbox system works well, many prefer to limit its use to vacant houses. Customs differ by locality. In some areas, recent technology records the name of every agent who opens the box.

A lockbox on the door has helped sell many a home because of the ease and spontaneity it adds to house hunting.

126. What information do I owe to potential buyers?

Because other people will make important financial decisions based on the information contained in your listing, it is essential that the details be as accurate as possible. Your listing agent should check lot size against your deed or survey, which will also yield a legal description of the property. Lot size can also be verified with the taxing authorities, which will furnish the true tax figures. Your tax bill may be misleadingly small (in some localities) if you are a veteran or a senior citizen or are affiliated with a religious organization. It may be inflated, on the other hand, because of special assessments or unpaid municipal water bills.

Unless you are sure about the square footage of your home, it's best to measure before putting the property on the market. The agent can help you use outside measurements, not counting basement or attic space. It's customary to list finished spaces as "plus 400-square-foot finished basement" or "heated porch." While you're outside, show the agent your property lines.

The old rule of caveat emptor, let the buyer beware, no longer has the force it once did in the sale of real estate. You and the agent can both be held responsible for misrepresentation. Not only must you answer questions truthfully but you must volunteer information on any hidden defect or major problem, particularly if it involves health or safety.

A hidden defect is one that is not readily apparent in a normal prudent inspection. You are not required to say, "Come back here, you didn't notice the big crack in the living room ceiling" because the prospects could have noticed it for themselves. You should point out, however, that the septic tank is inadequate for the size of the house and requires frequent attention. If you do not do this, you may be storing up trouble for the future.

State laws requiring sellers to reveal hidden defects vary, ranging from old-fashioned caveat emptor (on its way out) to an elaborate disclosure form required of all sellers in some states.

In many areas, you are required to have past utility bills available to buyers. If you haven't kept them, your fuel supplier will furnish copies. Information about insulation is also welcomed by buyers.

For mortgages on houses built before 1978, buyers usually must sign acknowledgement that they have received specific written lead paint warnings. The notice must be given before a sales contract is signed.

At the time of listing, reveal all liens (financial claims) against your property. Your mortgage or trust deed is probably the largest lien. Others may include back taxes, mechanics' liens (filed perhaps for that driveway work you refused to pay for) or personal judgments. Your agent and your lawyer will investigate problem areas.

You must also disclose, at the time you list the property, all you know about easements (the neighbor's right to use your driveway), code violations (you know the plumbing isn't up to standards) and zoning variances (the house isn't really zoned for an attic apartment, but the city hasn't bothered you). If you are involved in a boundary dispute with a neighbor, mention it now.

127. What things must I leave with the home?

All property is divided into two classes: real and personal. Real estate consists of the land and whatever is attached to it. Personal property (chattels) is movable. The tree growing on your land is part of the real estate. When it is cut into lumber, it becomes personal property that can be carried away.

In the opposite manner, chattels can become part of the real estate. A bathtub in a store is personal property that can be loaded into your station wagon. Take it home and hook it up to your plumbing system and it becomes part of the real estate. It becomes, in fact, a *fixture,* which is a special term for chattels that have become real property.

You need to know this because many disputes in real estate transactions center around what does and does not remain with the property. In general, chattels may be taken away; fixtures must remain. To avoid argument, remove certain items before anyone views the property. If you plan to keep the large mirror in the hall or—most commonly—the special dining room chandelier, the simplest solution is to replace the item before showing the house. What prospects don't see, they can't want. If you are not going to do this, state clearly in writing, at the time you list, that you reserve the right to remove the rosebushes, the window air conditioner or anything else a buyer might assume stays with the property.

Items that most often give trouble are lighting fixtures, drapes, satellite dishes, basketball backboards, swing sets and wood stoves. The law holds that all items should remain that are permanently attached, arc adapted to the use for which they were installed and were intended to remain. It's best to forestall arguments.

Carpeting usually remains if it is attached to the floor. Appliances are removable unless they are built-in. Even if you are willing to leave free-standing appliances, do not mention them in your listing; they may come in handy as bargaining tools later.

If you try to sell the house with its furniture, you eliminate many potential buyers. Offer the house alone, noting that you would sell it with furnishings if so requested. You can always hold a professionally run tag sale for the furniture later.

128. What goes on a supplementary fact sheet?

Besides the information on the listing form, other data can be of value to house hunters. Your agent may prepare a standard information sheet.

If you are selling on your own, an information sheet is essential and will contain the same facts that an agent's listing contract would include. Putting one together is a fascinating desktop-publishing project for the owner of a personal computer.

Room sizes and floor plans can be noted on your fact sheet. Mention carpet and tile colors. Describe the insulation, which is of ever-increasing interest. Utility bills should be summarized, noting nonrecurring expenses ("the water bill is high because we filled the pool twice").

This is the place to describe particular features you are proud of and to list nearby schools, bus lines and shopping centers. (You may want to omit from the list neighborhood places of worship, which could be interpreted as an attempt to attract certain prospective buyers, in violation of fair housing laws.)

Ask your neighbors whether they would regard it as an invasion of privacy if you describe them in your information sheet, noting where they work and the ages of their children.

A small picture of your home can go at the top of the sheet, making it easier for buyers to remember which property was yours.

129. What if I have friends who say they may be interested in buying?

If you delay listing with an agent, you could lose valuable time waiting for your friends' decision. You have two ways to handle this situation. You can turn over their names to the listing agent, or you can request a statement that no commission will be due if the property is sold to a particular person. Many brokers will honor a request to exempt specific purchasers from the listing contract.

Sometimes it's wise to add "no commission due if sold to Mr. and Mrs. Procrastinator *within the next 60 days*"—the idea being that if they haven't signed a contract within that time, you may want to turn your agent loose on them.

The listing contract should be signed by all owners of the property, and in some states, this may include a spouse who is not an owner. A salesperson also signs the listing contract on behalf of the broker with whom you enter into the agreement.

It can be instructive, at this point, to list the reasons you originally purchased this particular home. Perhaps you bought because of the nearby bus line; then you bought a second car and haven't thought about public transportation since. But your original reasons may influence other buyers. Give this information to your agent or use it yourself in writing ads for the property.

130. I'm selling on my own. What should I do about the agent who wants to show the house to "just one buyer"?

If you're hearing from a buyers' broker, you can make it clear that you will not pay any commission and that on that basis, you will allow the house to be shown.

On the other hand—depending on how long you've been trying to sell and how badly you need to move—you might offer to pay half the firm's regular commission if the property is sold to that one specific prospect. This is fair because the broker would have had no expense for advertising.

In either case, get the understanding down on paper and signed by you and the broker before the potential buyer enters your home.

Chapter 17

Pricing Your Home To Sell

If you offered your home for sale at $2 million, it would never sell (or it would remain on the market until inflation caught up with your price). If you asked $10 for it, you'd have a sale before your advertisement even hit the papers. (The supervisor of the newspaper's classified ad department would be at your door five minutes after you called.)

So you need only search for the figure, somewhere between $10 and $2 million, that will attract buyers and at the same time bring you the most money. One point is clear: If you can sell for $10 in five minutes and for $2 million in 20 years, it is obvious that time and money are related in real estate sales.

If you are under no pressure to sell, you have the luxury of exploring the market, experimenting with price and accepting an offer without pressure. This process is likely to yield the highest price.

131. What should I do if I'm under a deadline to sell?

In that situation, a no-nonsense price, slightly less than true market value, will bring immediate action.

A one-day sale, though, does not meet the standards set for fair market value of property. The concept of fair market value comes from the field of appraising.

Fair market value has been defined as the most probable price a property will bring if it has been widely exposed on the market, if sufficient time is allowed to find an informed buyer and if neither party is under undue duress. Fair market value may or may not be the same as the eventual sales price.

Pricing your property involves an attempt to estimate fair market value, depending on circumstances.

132. Is the assessment a good guide to asking price?

An assessment, the result of a specific type of appraisal, is set by the taxing authorities as a basis for levying property taxes. No matter how often assessments are reviewed and how sincere an effort is made to keep them in line with market value, assessed value is seldom a dependable guide.

Some sellers have other misconceptions about where to start estimating value. Here are factors to ignore:

Your Cost. How much you paid for your home has nothing to do with how much you can sell it for. Suppose you received your home as a gift; must you then give it away?

Your Investment in Improvements. You put in that purple kitchen because you enjoyed it, but you are not likely to find a buyer who feels that the house is worth $20,000 more because of it. Certain viewers may even calculate the cost of tearing it out and replacing it with something in fuchsia.

Reproduction Cost.   The money it would take to dupli-cate your home, building it from scratch, is its reproduction cost. Reproduction cost is usually estimated for property insur-ance purposes, but it is of little value in setting sale price, except for a newly built house.

Your Needs.   Also irrelevant to the proper asking price for your property is the amount of money you must take out of it. You may require $40,000 net in order to buy your next home. That fact may influence your decision to sell or not to sell: You cannot move unless you have the $40,000. But it is not the basis for pricing your present home.

Your problems are not the buyer's concern. The public is looking at various houses and comparing prices. Supply and demand, operating in the open market, will set the value for your property. Your home can be priced properly only if it is considered in competition with other property.

Emotion.   You cannot charge for sentiment, for the fact that your daughter took her first steps on the patio and your son had a clubhouse behind the garage. Your emotions can lead to serious mistakes in setting the asking price.

In the case of divorce, for example, emotions can play havoc with price. If one party is impatient to leave town and the other isn't getting the money anyway, a buyer is likely to pick up a bargain.

Dramatic family changes may produce sellers who just want to turn their backs on their situations. Still, you should aim for a sale at fair market value, without letting emotions influence your listing price.

133. What things do count when I set my price?

These are the factors that you should consider:

Urgency of the Sale.   You will reduce your asking price in proportion to your need for a quick sale. If foreclosure threatens, offer a bargain price right from the start. If you must leave the house vacant, add up what it would cost you to carry it for three or four extra months—mortgage payments, insurance, taxes, utilities and lost income from the equity you will have tied up in the house. You might be better off listing at less than market value rather than incurring those expenses and in the end selling at a lower price anyhow.

Competition.   If few homes are for sale in your desirable location, yours can be marked up a bit for scarcity. If, on the other hand, a local plant recently moved out of town and the market is flooded with houses in your price range, you will have to discount to find a buyer. Your agent can tell you whether you are in a buyer's or seller's market at the moment. If you are selling on your own, investigate local unemployment figures; they are a good quick guide.

Special Financing.   If your home has a large FHA or VA loan that can be assumed at a rate below current levels, your mortgage is probably the most valuable part of the property. The house is likely to bring a premium from a buyer willing to exchange a higher total price for savings in interest payments in the years ahead. Much the same is true, in a difficult mortgage market, if you are willing to hold the loan yourself.

Comparable sales are the key to proper pricing. Nothing matters as much as "comps," which are completed transactions as similar to yours as possible. The homes selected for comparison should be physically near because no single factor determines value more surely than location. The sales should also be recent; two-year-old transactions have almost no meaning in today's volatile market. And they should be close in style, size and condition to your property—the closer the better.

Your agent can furnish figures on comparables; at least three are recommended, and if six close comps are available, so much the better. Pay little attention to neighborhood scuttlebutt; sellers exaggerate the amount they received, and buyers minimize the price paid.

The agent probably will not offer you a "free appraisal." Experts feel that if it's free, it isn't an appraisal. You will receive instead a comparative market analysis. This computation lists several recent nearby sales, notes how long each was on the market and how close the asking price was to the eventual sale figure and then compares the houses with yours. The process is a simple version of the market approach, the technique most often used for formal residential appraisals.

Besides considering the comparative market analysis, study a complete list of homes currently on the market in your area. Buyers will choose homes to view from that group. Consider your property through their eyes, and judge how your asking price compares—whether it would attract you before you knew the property.

Study ads for houses in your area to build a general background on the current market. A comparison of the average prices of comparable sales with the average asking prices of similar homes not yet sold can give you an idea of how much bargaining seems to be built-in. Community custom varies in this matter. Your agent may have a computer printout of past sales, with asking prices and sale prices listed for easy comparison.

Bargaining practices vary with individual preferences. Some sellers detest bargaining and list at firm, rock-bottom prices. Others tack on a few thousand dollars just to see whether they'll be lucky. Nevertheless, there is often a discernible trend, giving you a clue to what the average buyer might expect. You may find sale prices averaging from 5 percent to 10 percent less than listing prices.

Remember that owning real estate means controlling it, and that includes setting your asking price. Your agent may be eager to persuade you to set a reasonable price or, on the other hand, may avoid making any recommendation at all. In the end, the decision is entirely yours.

134. How much can I expect to net from my sale?

Know the definition of equity: the amount of money you will realize if you sell your home at fair market value and pay all the liens (claims) against it. Equity is often the sales price of the house minus the amount owed on the mortgage.

Although you cannot set your list price on the basis of the amount of money you need to receive, it is wise to estimate what you may net and what your selling expenses may be as you price the house.

Depending on your financing, the buyer's loan, state law and other factors, your costs of selling are likely to be these:

- Commission
- Points (see Chapter 21). Your agent can orient you on points, taking into account the current mortgage market.
- Adjustments. You may owe the buyer for unpaid property taxes or be owed money for fuel oil left in the tank. Items like these will be adjusted at the time of closing.
- Legal fees. These may include your lawyer's fee, title insurance and escrow or title company charges. Your main responsibility is to prove clear and marketable title.
- Transfer taxes. In some states, this item must be paid by the seller, no matter how other costs are shared.
- Inspections. Depending on local custom, you may be expected to pay for code inspections, a termite check or a land survey.
- Special assessments. If, for example, your property is being assessed because of new sidewalks or similar neighborhood improvements, you might be asked to pay this lien in a lump sum at closing.
- Present liens. These include your mortgage and other claims or judgments of record against the property.

- Prepayment penalties. Not too many mortgages have them these days, but if you will be paying off your loan at the closing, find out whether you face any prepayment charges.
- Required repairs. Your agent can help judge whether the FHA, the VA or a lending institution will require that you make specific repairs or bring your home up to code. The matter should be considered when you set your price.

Unexpected Credits.   You may receive monies at closing that you don't anticipate. Fuel oil reimbursement is an example. In some states, property taxes are paid in advance, and adjustments may result in a sizable refund to you. Prepaid insurance should also be refunded. You may have established an escrow account at your lending institution, with money collected in advance for tax and insurance expenses you will no longer owe. This sum is returned to you.

135. What's the harm in trying to sell for a higher price at first if I'm willing to come down?

At any given time, a large pool of buyers is on the market, and these buyers constitute your best prospects. It will take approximately three months to replace them with an equal number of newcomers to the market.

If your home is overpriced, you will lose the advantage of this ready group of buyers. They are accustomed to comparing properties and may refuse even to view yours. You and your agent may know that you will sell for less, but the buyers may not know. Fiduciary duty prohibits your agent from telling them this or advertising the fact. So your overpriced property receives little attention.

Surveys show that the longer a house is on the market, the greater is the discount from listing price when it finally sells. The buying public eventually sets an accurate price. The overpriced house lingers on the market, requiring a price adjustment before it attracts a buyer.

"We can always come down" is a phrase agents don't enjoy hearing. It implies a slow start, wasted advertisements, unpleasant discussions with the homeowner and, eventually, a shopworn property. Knowledgeable buyers ask how long a house has been on the market and why it hasn't sold. Even when the agent explains that only the price was wrong, buyers may remain suspicious.

If you have your heart set on trying a high price "just to see," first work out a written plan to drop the price at intervals: If the house hasn't attracted enough attention in two weeks, the price will be cut to a certain level. If you haven't had an offer within a month, you will lower it again. Make sure you will be down to real market value within six weeks. Such a commitment at the beginning ensures a logical, stress-free handling of the problem.

Even if lightning strikes and an out-of-town buyer, unfamiliar with the market, agrees to pay an inflated price, trouble lies ahead. You may then be faced with the question of "whether the house will appraise." The buyer's lending institution will send an appraiser to estimate the property's value. You and the buyer may have agreed that the house is worth $195,000. But if the bank appraiser doesn't agree, you have a problem. The mortgage loan will be offered on the basis of that lower figure, and the buyer may not be able (or willing) to complete the purchase.

136. What happens if I price the property too low?

The first serious consequence of underpricing, of course, is that you will lose money. Even the most experienced agent is fooled, occasionally, when a house that seemed properly priced suddenly turns out to be a "hot" listing.

What are the signs? One is an immediate rush of calls from other offices either to your agent asking how to show the property or directly to you requesting appointments. Another sure sign is a jam-packed open house. Prospects pile up in the living room, waiting their turns to see the property, while your agent phones the office for reinforcements.

Whether using an agent or selling on your own, you may receive several purchase offers immediately if you have under-priced. An experienced agent may advise a prospective buyer to offer more than the asking price so that if that buyer's proposal is presented at the same time as several others, it stands a good chance of acceptance.

If such a situation develops, consult your attorney immediately. It appears that a mistake has been made in the asking price; can you now refuse a full-price offer? Can you raise your list price? Obtain legal advice as quickly as you can.

In the absence of any offers, it is possible to raise your asking price immediately. Your agent or your lawyer will know the procedure, although it is seldom used.

One final point to be considered in pricing your property is the $10,000 barrier. There is very little difference in buyers' reactions to a house priced at $147,000 compared with one priced at $149,000, and a great deal of difference between houses priced at $149,000 and $151,000. If you are wavering over a few extra thousand and the higher figure will take you just above $150,000, remember that you are automatically cutting out of your buying public all those who told their agents, "Don't show me anything over $150,000." You could be eliminating the best prospects for your home. Consider $149,999.99 instead. It is just as useful in attracting buyers as $149,000 would be.

137. Do I need a professional paid appraisal?

The money invested in a professional appraisal may be worth spending in the beginning, or later if you and the agent are stymied as to the proper price.

An appraisal can be a valuable bargaining tool during contract negotiations with your buyer. Although it is simply an estimate—albeit an informed, skilled one—the buyer usually accepts it as impartial, almost scientific proof of value, as indeed the courts do.

Most sellers, though, rely on their agents' comparative market analysis figures. If the agent is experienced in your particular neighborhood, the recommended price you'll get that way is probably as accurate as any elaborate appraisal.

The seller who doesn't use a broker is usually advised to pay a few hundred dollars for a complete written appraisal done by a professional appraiser with a designation, an appraiser's license or certification—someone with special study and qualification. (Make it clear that you need only a simple written report; you don't want to pay for a 30-page dissertation with floor plans and photographs of the neighborhood.) You have little to gain from selling your home in one day because you've priced it too low.

138. If I sell on my own, can I ask real estate brokers for free advice on the matter?

Yes and no.

It's manifestly unfair to mislead an agent by asking for a market analysis on the pretense that you plan to list the property. But what if you were up front about it? You might call several firms, explain that you intend to try marketing the house yourself and ask whether they are willing to confer with you on that understanding.

Even an oral off-hand opinion will require an hour's preparation time on the agent's part and another hour traveling to your home and inspecting it. Understandably, some brokers will refuse to donate their time and expertise to your project.

Others, though, may be willing to provide the service, hoping to make a friend in the process. Some brokers believe that nine out of ten FSBOs eventually do list, and they're glad for a chance to meet you and try to sell their services.

Chapter 18

*P*reparing Your Home To Shine on the Market

*L*et's talk about buying a used car. Assume you're just looking for dependable transportation.

You go to see a blue car—at least you think it's blue; hard to tell under the dirt. You can't judge the tire treads because they're caked with mud.

You sit in the driver's seat—gingerly, because the upholstery is stained. The dome light doesn't work, and the ashtray spills butts. There's a dirty coffee mug on the dashboard. You can't test the seatbelt because it's tucked away. The back seat is full of mashed crayons, juice cartons and stuck-on bubble gum.

Remember, all you're looking for is transportation. For all we know, the car has been well maintained. Why should the way the owner lives be anyone's business?

But most buyers would just walk away. In the end, the owner wouldn't get what the car is really worth. To bring full value, it could have been taken for a complete doll-up and a new fuse for the dome light before the ad went in the paper.

No seller should conceal defects, but there's nothing wrong with putting your best foot forward.

139. How do I begin to polish my property?

Start by asking your agent for suggestions. You may have learned to compensate for the broken front step and no longer even notice it. The salesperson's practiced eye, on the other hand, can pinpoint spots that need attention.

If you are selling on your own, call in a blunt friend. You want someone who will view your home with a fresh eye.

What you are looking for is advice on which features can be inexpensively improved and which may be left alone. You can spend little or no money and enhance your property markedly. Attend to all those items that require no outlay.

If you feel unequal to the job, don't worry. There are cleaning services that will go through your whole place in a few hours, organizing and polishing. After all, when you move you'll have to clear stuff out anyhow.

Assuming you care about getting full value and selling promptly, polishing your home will be well worth the trouble. But if you don't care, don't bother. In the end, any house will sell, in any condition or location, if the price is low enough.

140. What should I do on the outside?

Prospective buyers will probably park across the street—that's where the agent will guide them. Sit there in your own car and see how the house strikes you. Remember, your property will never get a second chance to make a first impression. Is the lawn as near perfect as possible, or could it benefit from a little fertilizer? Are the bushes trimmed? Is your garage door closed? One detail can make a great difference. Of course it's too late to landscape, but in season, a few showy annuals can add sparkle to your front lawn at small expense.

Your fences and gates should be in good repair, possibly repainted. Downspouts and gutters should be firmly attached; house numbers need checking also. Don't forget your driveway; remove unsightly oil stains and fill in small cracks. Old cars or a camper that lives in your driveway may need another home for the interim.

No matter how attached you may be to your flamingos, wooden whirligigs, decorative eagles and artificial flowers, all such items are a matter of personal taste. Your exterior will look more spacious and serene without them; store them neatly in your garage for the duration.

Consider your trash cans. Can you keep them concealed at all times? If not, make sure they're clean and neat.

You already have enough assignments for a full Saturday's work, and you haven't reached the front door yet!

141. What needs attention in the house?

Stand at your front door where the buyer will stand, and look around. Do the porch light and the doorbell work? It goes without saying that your screen door is in good condition and the muddy pawprints beside the door have been scrubbed. The glass panels in the door sparkle, as does every window in the house. Even if you don't paint any other part of the house, consider freshening the front entrance. A bit of black paint can do wonders for a worn threshold.

Front Hall. The front hall or foyer should be free of clutter, and you may add a vase of (fresh) flowers or another welcoming touch—just one. In the front hall closet, remove out-of-season clothing and dead storage. All your closets will look larger if they are orderly and uncrowded.

Living Room. Lay a fire in the fireplace, consider whether the carpets could benefit from a shampoo and remove unnecessary pieces of large furniture. Even though you cherish them, put away personal possessions such as trophies, artificial flowers, family pictures and political and religious items. Most living rooms can be improved if two-thirds of their distracting accessories are removed. You want a room that buyers can try on for size, with plenty of space for their personal items. Pack away breakable and particularly valuable items. After all, you will be doing that when you move, anyway. Pack-rat homeowners have been known to strip a crowded house of half their possessions and rent a self-storage commercial locker.

Although there is no hard-and-fast rule about repainting your home's interior, you should attend to cracks and water stains on the ceilings. A stain may go back five years to the time when Uncle Erwin let the tub overflow. But even if you try to explain it, a buyer will remain nervous about your plumbing system. Simply repaint the ceiling. You must not cover your problems in an attempt to hide them, but neither do you owe the buyer a complete history of your troubles with Uncle Erwin.

As for small cracks in walls or ceilings, they may have been there for decades, but some buyers will be sure they indicate danger of imminent collapse. Cracked window panes leave an impression that the house has been neglected; attend to them before anyone views the property.

Kitchen.   Kitchens and baths are the rooms that traditionally sell houses. It seldom pays to remodel in anticipation of selling, so the kitchen will have to remain basically as it is. You can, however, check a number of items. Leaky faucets should be repaired and stains bleached out of the sink. To show off your expanse of kitchen counters, remove most items, leaving only one or two decorative pieces or basic appliances.

Even if your stove is not included in the sale, someone will be sure to open the oven; have it spotless. A greasy oven is a real turn-off, and the impression it conveys will extend to the rest of the house. Glass doors on ovens, toaster ovens and microwaves should be polished.

In insect-prone areas, keep extermination up to date. Remove sticky fingerprints everywhere. If you want to invest a small amount of money, try bright, inexpensive curtains, or dress up your cupboards with modern knobs.

Bathrooms. Looking at other people's bathrooms can be an unappealing process; make it as easy as possible. Take a good look at your shower curtain; a stained one can be replaced with a sparkling, inexpensive new one in a solid neutral color. White is always a good choice—no mermaids or flamingos. Consider replacing a chipped toilet seat as well. Bring in a potted plant. Check grout around your tub and shower. Remove tub mats. Buy a set of solid-colored towels and washcloths to be set out at the last minute before the house is shown.

This is a good time to clean out the medicine chest; the inside can be painted with a few minutes' effort.

Bedrooms. In bedrooms, straighten closet clutter, remove large or crowded pieces of furniture if possible and put out your best bedspreads; make sure, again, that the windows are spotless.

Throughout the Entire House. Replace burned-out light bulbs. Wash doorknobs and light switches. Check staircase treads and tighten railings. Make it easy for house hunters to use your attic and basement stairs, which should be free of clutter.

If you are not a plant person, consider borrowing some particularly full and healthy ones from friends. Just a few plants or trees, judiciously placed around the house, add warmth.

This is a good time to hose down your basement floor and garage. Your electric box will be inspected, so clean off cobwebs and dust.

If you've already left town and can't attend to these tasks, ask your agent to arrange for a cleaning crew to go through the interior, and to supervise lawn mowing, snow shoveling, heating or air-conditioning and the like. It's penny-wise and pound-foolish to cut corners at this point and an imposition to depend on your friends or ex-neighbors. You need to be sure the property is shiny clean and always ready for viewers.

142. How much should I spend on my home when it's going up for sale?

Spend as little as possible.

Except in rare instances, it is unwise to invest much cash in improving a house that is going on the market. It is usually impossible to recoup the outlay by raising your price. Eliminate major improvements from your plans.

If you are prepared, though, to spend some money on a fix-up, your best investment—after soap—is probably paint. Take a tip from the merchandisers of new model homes: Paint every room the same color to make the house look larger. A light neutral shade is the best choice. This is not the time to strive for spectacular results, for you want your home to harmonize with almost anyone's furniture. Don't forget, when painting, to do the insides of closets also.

If some of your rooms have shabby rugs, perhaps old-style shag in vibrant green or orange, throw them out. The bare floor will probably appeal to buyers more. Or you can shop for remnants at any rug store. You'll be amazed at how inexpensive large rugs can be when you're not concerned about exact size or particular weave—and how much they'll dress up your rooms. Just stick to light beige or gray.

One most-for-your-money job is resealing a blacktop driveway to give the outside of the house a crisp, clean appearance. Ambitious homeowners may go on from there to sand and refinish floors.

If your home features what appraisers tactfully call casual housekeeping, your agent is in a delicate situation. The broker knows that time and again such a house remains on the market for months and eventually sells for thousands of dollars less than its real value. But suggestions that a house needs cleaning and tidying are difficult to put politely.

Take seriously, therefore, any suggestion by your broker that you consider a professional cleaning service. If you have doubts about your housekeeping, ask your agent, or that blunt friend, whether a professional job is indicated.

As you look forward to the first showing of your home, gather your fact sheets, copies of the listing material and past fuel and utility bills. If you have pictures of the back lawn when it was blanketed with snow or the front lawn with the cherry trees in blossom, display them prominently so that prospects can appreciate the beauty of your home in every season.

A home warranty is a nice selling point and gives the buyer a sense of security. Warranties typically cover appliances (which may already be under warranty), heating, plumbing and electrical systems. They do not, however, cover structural defects. Sometimes the homeowner is charged for labor or travel time or must pay a fairly stiff deductible before the warranty kicks in. In addition, at least one major company in the field has recently gone into bankruptcy. Even so, offering a warranty sounds good enough that it's probably worth your spending a few hundred dollars.

143. What should the ad for my home emphasize?

One of the agent's first tasks is to write advertising for your property. You may be asked to help or to suggest phrases, if you like that kind of challenge. It can be useful to mention your own reasons for buying the house.

If you are placing your own advertisements, you may be shocked when the first bills come in. Remember that long ads are not necessarily better than short ones. Buyers do not catch fire from lists that simply catalog the house's features, and they may even skip over long ads. They read the bewildering variety of offerings not to select but to reject houses. Too much information may include the one fact that eliminates your home from the list. Leave them something to call about.

Your ad should include location, number of bedrooms and baths, price level and one or two picture-making phrases. "For Sale by Owner" is always an attention-getter, and so, for your initial ad, is "First Offering Today."

Brokers are sometimes vague on prices in their ads because they want contact with as many potential buyers as possible. You might as well list your price, though, to cut down on phone calls from those who can't afford your home. Never say you are *asking* $160,000, though, as that signals that you are ready to settle for less. You may be, but there's no use giving away your negotiating advantage.

Be careful that your ad does not violate fair housing laws by suggesting a preference based on illegal discrimination. Your newspaper should have guidelines. Mentioning nearby churches, for example, or the ethnic composition of your neighborhood, could put you in violation.

If you do sell through an agent, the chances of the right buyer calling on your particular ad are remote. In the end, your buyer probably will have first contacted the broker about another property. Although advertising represents the largest item in the broker's budget, it accounts for only one-third of the sales. Most sales come from referrals or other contacts, For Sale signs and the firm's backlog of purchasers.

Speaking of For Sale signs, if you sell on your own, check any local sign ordinances or subdivision restrictions before you invest in a handsome custom-printed sign.

Chapter 19

*S*howing Off Your Home to Potential Buyers

*P*ut a gingerbread mix in the oven, throw out the kids and gather last year's utility bills. The buyers are coming, the buyers are coming!

144. As a FSBO, are there precautions I should take about showing my home?

Put the words "By Appointment Only" and a phone number on your For Sale sign. You don't want to invite in anyone who knocks on your door; if people do this, ask them to phone for an appointment. When you receive the call, ask for the caller's own phone number "so I can call you back and confirm." This provides a certain amount of identification ahead of time, for safety's sake.

The advance appointment gives you time to prepare your home and to arrange for another adult to be in the house with you if you wish.

When you give prospects directions to your home, consider the most attractive approach. There's no law that says you must direct them past the town dump if the route through the park works as well.

Right after your house goes on the market, watch out for bargain hunters on the prowl for unsophisticated FSBOs. They will be less interested in the house itself than in finding out whether you will sell with no down payment and whether you will take back financing (discussed in Chapter 21). Such buyers often cannot qualify for bank loans because they have poor credit or insufficient income.

Before you place your first advertisement, you will have calculated the amount of cash and income a buyer would need to qualify for a mortgage loan on your property (see Chapter 21). You will not, therefore, invite in everyone who inquires. Apply the same standards to every caller to make sure you observe human rights law. You have a right to ask name, phone number and present address and whether the caller rents or has another house to sell. You may also ask about employment and income. The prospect may, of course, refuse to answer. Then you'll have to play it by ear.

Here's a handy list of things to do when selling on your own:

- Retain a lawyer who specializes in real estate.
- Visit open houses in your neighborhood for three weeks.
- Clip classified ads for houses in your neighborhood.
- Phone agents for information on the ads you clip.
- Interview at least three local brokers (see Chapter 14). Be frank about not wanting to list yet.
- Polish your home to show it at its best (see Chapter 18).
- Ask your lawyer for a blank copy of a typical purchase offer.
- Prepare fact sheets on your property.
- Prepare a lawn sign.
- Place your classified ad. Buyers need to know neighborhood, style of house, number of rooms and bedrooms (and baths and garages, if more than one) and price or price range. Keep the ad short.
- Never answer "How much would you take?" directly.
- Ask serious prospects to bring you a credit report.

- When you receive an oral offer you like, ask your lawyer to prepare a contract acceptable to both parties.
- Follow the buyer's mortgage application process, and check at least once a week—or have your lawyer do so—to see how it's going.

145. How do brokers arrange to show my property?

If the broker has a prospect waiting in the wings for property like yours, arrangements for the first showing may be made as soon as you sign the listing. In areas with a strong Multiple Listing Service, you can expect to hear from other brokers soon after your properly priced house goes on the market.

Agents always try to arrange appointments by phone. If they are setting up several houses for a buyer to see, they might say, "We'll be over between two and three o'clock," rather than promising to ring the bell at 2:30 PM.

Don't hold out for too much advance notice. You could eliminate one of the most promising prospects—the transferred employee who is in town for a few hours, needs to find a place today and wants to come right over. Try to say yes. After all, it will take the salesperson half an hour to drive over, and you can accomplish a great deal of last-minute polishing in the interim. Make the house as freely available as possible.

Even if you have left a key with the lister so that the house can be shown while you are at work, most agents will still phone ahead to see whether anyone is at home. Because they may come in while you are absent, you'll have to see that the place is tidy before you leave each day. In the event someone does enter, you should find a business card left behind, ideally noting the time of the visit.

146. What should I do about people who simply knock on the door?

Even with a broker's sign out front, people may knock on your door asking if they may see the house. Tell them pleasantly that it is being shown only by the office whose telephone number is on the sign outside. Do not admit any strangers; you retained an agent to avoid just such situations. Chances are slim that random inquirers are really qualified to buy. If, on the other hand, they are good prospects, they should receive professional treatment from the start. A slight difficulty in getting into the house will only make it more desirable.

Once in a while, an agent may ring your doorbell without phoning in advance: "I was just driving by with some folks who noticed the sign and like the looks of the house. They won't be here tomorrow; they're waiting in the car to hear if they can come in."

If possible, welcome them. The broker knows what they can afford and what they seek; if the agent thinks it's worth the trouble, it probably is. You can gain a few minutes to tidy up by suggesting that they inspect the exterior first.

Prospects who enter a house this way are already half sold. They are grateful for your cooperation, and the sense of discovery and unplanned adventure in such a showing often results in a sale.

147. How does an open house work?

The first weekend after your home goes on the market is probably the most productive time to tap the existing pool of buyers and to allow buyers and brokers to view the home without the bother of an appointment.

You—or your agent—advertise the open house and put out signs inviting all comers to visit during specified hours. It's helpful if the open house takes place when there are others in the neighborhood, usually on Saturday or Sunday. Some localities restrict signs; in other areas, balloons, flags and streamers lend a festive atmosphere.

After all the work of preparation, you will be longing to see the fun. If you have an agent, though, you'll probably be asked to leave before the open house starts. If you can't bear to go away, visit a neighbor so you can see what happens.

Unless your home is strikingly underpriced, don't expect hordes of visitors. And remember that fewer than one house in 20 is sold through an open house. The agent is experienced in handling visitors and will probably insist that they identify themselves and sign in. For the agent, it's an opportunity to meet buyers.

If you run the open house yourself, have someone else with you on the premises. Always ask people to sign in, and ask for identification. If you have several prospects at once, have them wait in the living room or, in good weather, outside while you escort one couple at a time through the house.

Your neighbors, who have always been curious about what's in your cupboards and attic, may show up somewhat shame-facedly at the first open house. It is wise to welcome them and even to have invited them. Neighbors may have friends or relatives who have always wanted to live nearby. An agent, of course, has an extra motive for being cordial, hoping to produce a successful sale and to be remembered when it's time to list the next house on the street.

After all the preparation you've put in during the past few weeks, what more can be done?

Plenty—whether for an open house or a private showing. Go through the house and raise every window shade. Draw the drapes back from those spotless windows. A bright house looks larger and more cheerful.

Turn on lights from top to bottom, even in the daytime. If you've ever gone through a builder's model home, you know how much extra charm a living room gains from shaded lamps and how a chandelier adds sparkle. Buyers shouldn't have to grope for the pullcord in the gloomy corner of the basement, and they should find your attic stairs well lighted.

Your house can appeal to all five senses as much as it can to rational inspection. Consider the sound level. Stop your dishwasher or clothes dryer in midcycle and check for other noisy appliances. If you want to leave your stereo set on, play neutral, easy-listening music, very softly. You are trying, after all, to set up a seduction scene.

The beds are made, of course, with your best spreads, and every room is as tidy as possible. Toilet seats are down, and those new towels have replaced the family ones. This doesn't mean there should be no signs of life—if you have fine linen and china, a beautifully set table adds appeal.

The subtle fragrance of onion and bay leaf from a pot roast simmering on the back burner won't hurt at all. Homeowners have been known to put a cake in the oven every time a prospect was on the way or to simmer a cinnamon stick for a few minutes. If, on the other hand, a smoker lives in your home, empty ashtrays and spray air freshener at the last moment. These days, agents report that some buyers won't even enter a house if they can tell the owner is a heavy smoker.

On any day that isn't sweltering, start a fire to dramatize your open hearth. If you regard a wood fire as a nuisance, buy pressed logs. One will burn alone and add a cozy glow throughout an afternoon's open house, leaving very little ash. And the viewers won't have to wonder if the fireplace works.

148. Why don't brokers want the owner present during a showing?

No matter how charming your children and pets, getting them out of the house during viewings is an absolute must. Set up an emergency routine. On two minutes' notice, your kids should be able to corral Rover, put him on a leash, turn off the television, and dash out the back door for sanctuary in a neighbor's kitchen.

It's important that the house be as empty as possible and free from distractions. House hunting is confusing and tiring work.

The buyers are probably looking at several places within a few hours, trying to fix each in their minds. Ideally, they like to wander and explore, trying the place on for size, perhaps pretending it's already theirs.

Falling in love with a house is like falling in love with a person, and three's a crowd. Your role is to be pleasant and unobtrusive, if not downright unavailable. This spares your feelings and the buyers'.

It's difficult to watch strangers go through your home. You might be surprised by the strength of your emotional reaction to a random word of criticism. You would probably be upset by the buyers who never get farther than your front hall or who whiz through in one minute flat. The agent is used to it and knows that if buyers are searching for an eat-in kitchen or dead-end living room, they look for that first, cross your house off the list if it isn't there and save their energy for the next house.

With you watching, prospects are inhibited about opening closets, trying out windows, stroking the banister and performing all those get-acquainted gestures that are the house-hunting equivalent of kicking the tires and slamming the doors of a new car.

Of course if you are showing the house yourself, you need to monitor prospects unobtrusively for security reasons. Study the description below of the broker's standard techniques.

149. How does an experienced broker show the house?

Buyers are on their way over, you've given the house its last-minute sparkle and you peek out the window as they pull up.

Broker and buyers probably travel in one car; this gives the broker more control and opportunity for conversation. It's customary to park across the street for a good view of your property. You may think they are taking an unreasonably long time to reach the front door. Remember that in good weather, many brokers make it a practice to show the outside first, building suspense for the home itself.

When the doorbell rings (aren't you glad you fixed it?), greet the buyers with a smile, wait to be introduced and then excuse yourself. "Don't bother with the lights; I'll take care of them later. If you need me, I'll be next door." There is a proper time for you to reappear (see Question 150), but consider first more reasons why you shouldn't hang around.

Potential buyers are reluctant to voice objections with you standing by. They can speak frankly to the broker, who knows whether the house might fit their needs and how to respond to their comments.

"That den is so tiny."

"Yes," agrees the broker, who would never contradict a valid observation. "You did say you're looking for a sewing room, though. I suppose it could be down on this floor instead of upstairs."

"You know, it might just do. Ben, come and look at this little room." When couples start showing the house to each other, the wise broker fades into the background.

Although you know your home, the agent knows these buyers. They've already looked at several properties today, they are remarkably suspicious about plumbing problems, they want a neighborhood full of kids and they need a long dining room wall for an heirloom breakfront.

An eager homeseller, full of nervous chatter, can blunder in several ways with these people. Proud of the new paint job, you might point out that the living room ceiling was just redone to get rid of an old stain from the time when crazy Uncle Erwin. . . . You'd never realize the needless anxiety this stirs up in some buyers.

If they ask about children in the neighborhood, you might voice your own attitude and reply, "They never bother me; you wouldn't know there were any around." And the buyers might conclude, perhaps wrongly, that your street lacks just the playmates they had hoped to find for their children.

As for that dining room, the broker won't say a single word while the buyers stand spellbound in the doorway, mentally placing their furniture against the long wall. If you stick around while a skilled broker shows your home, you may become nervous listening to the silence. But although the broker may not say much, he or she is listening very hard. Don't expect a stream of patter and salesmanship. A good broker uses skill and expertise to match buyer and house, then lets the place sell itself, putting in a few deft words where they will do the most good.

The agent tries never to argue and fades away discreetly when it becomes obvious that husband and wife need to confer in private. Such moments come as they begin to feel they may have found the right house, but neither can voice that conviction until they have compared notes. Your home showing is likely to involve a great deal of silence, which can be unnerving to a homeowner.

Another problem, if you join the group, is the simple matter of space. It's easy for stairways and halls to become crowded. The broker knows better than to enter small bedrooms with prospects.

If it's obvious that the couple might be really interested in your home, the broker may suggest that they go back through it once more, on their own. If they say "yes, we'd like to," you're close to an offer.

150. Should I ever meet prospective buyers?

If you've been over at the neighbor's house and now realize that these prospects have been in your home a long time (20 minutes or more), it may be helpful for you to put in an appearance.

The broker wants to begin and end the viewing in the most pleasant room: the living room (with the log burning on the hearth), the kitchen (with the cookies cooling on the counter) or the family room (with the bowl of polished apples on the television set). This is a good place for you to be discovered, sitting at your ease and prepared to answer questions. If the buyers are serious, they'll accept your invitation to sit down and chat.

You have valuable information for them: the age of neighbors' children, the time the school bus comes, how far it is to the library or the tennis club. Have your past utility bills available at this point, with exact costs detailed.

Remember that you must tell the truth about your property. Don't vouch for facts you're not sure of. They could come back to haunt you later. Refer troublesome questions back to the listing agent, who has probably heard them all before.

It will help in future negotiations if you and the buyers like one another, but you may notice some nervousness on the part of the broker if you become too informative at this point. The broker expects to act as a buffer between buyers and sellers.

Don't give a direct answer to any question about price.

The correct response to "Would you take $162,000?" is "I'll consider any written offers that come through my agent" (or, with no agent, "through my lawyer"). You should have asked your lawyer for a blank contract, which you can offer to a buyer who doesn't seem to know what to do next.

If you hear, "We need to move in by September; will you be out by then?" you might reply, "I'm sure we could work out the details."

This is also a poor time to discuss the sale of furniture or appliances. It's destructive to get hung up on small matters before the main event. If you've listed your stove and refrigerator as "negotiable" and are now asked if you'd leave them, say "that depends." The unspoken words here are "that depends on how close you come to my list price." To a question about whether you'd sell the pool table or the portable bar, a good response is "I thought I'd decide after the sale of the property is settled."

151. Can I expect a report about the showing?

If you were away from home while the property was shown, you can request that the broker call back later to report. Remember that the prospects have looked at several homes. If they decide to put in a purchase offer on one of the others, the agent will have a busy day or two, handling paperwork, negotiations, lenders and lawyers.

You can still ask for a call when the broker is free, to learn what the reaction was to your home. Request a frank report and you'll have valuable information on how your asking price strikes the buying public or suggestions on ways your home's appeal can be further enhanced.

Or perhaps you'll hear the real estate broker's ultimate compliment, "Your place shows well." And then, "They want to think it over. I may be getting in touch with your listing agent in a day or two with an offer."

Chapter 20

*A*rriving at the Best Contract for You

*Y*our real estate agent, always aware that you are the client to whom he or she owes full loyalty, aims to bring you and your buyer to what is legally known as a meeting of the minds. A successful agent develops valuable skills in negotiation, and a new salesperson will call upon the broker's experience in this matter. With both parties under stress, tact and diplomacy are called into action. The broker knows enough of law and finance to make suggestions for dealing with difficulties.

If you do not use a broker, you must deal directly with the would-be buyer. Always remember that oral agreements for the sale of real estate are not binding. The buyer could offer you $200,000 cash in front of five witnesses; you could shake hands on the deal and even accept a $20,000 deposit. And the buyer could still back out of the deal the next day and demand return of the deposit. As far as the law is concerned, there was no contract.

152. What about oral offers?

The statute of frauds demands that certain documents be in writing to be legally enforceable, and one of those is any contract for the sale of real property.

This makes negotiation particularly delicate, for you will only give yourself away if you engage in oral dickering.

Study the sample contract to purchase shown in Chapter 9 to familiarize yourself with typical provisions—don't try to use this specific one, of course. Obtain a contract suitable to your area from your broker or lawyer. If your agency uses one specially designed form for its transactions, also look at samples of other standard contracts used in your area.

Local custom dictates the manner in which the offer to purchase will be made. The form may be called an agreement to buy and sell, a binder receipt and option, an agreement to purchase, a sales contract or an offer and acceptance. Study it ahead of time so that when an offer comes in, you will be familiar with the standard provisions and can concentrate on the specific terms being offered.

It is helpful, also, if you familiarize yourself with the financing options open to potential buyers of your home. Chapter 21 discusses some alternatives. Because you will be asked to make decisions based on the buyers' plans for financing, be conversant with their choices. Your salesperson or attorney will have information on current financing opportunities.

Before any purchase offers come in, ask your lawyer for preliminary advice.

153. How is an offer presented?

If you are selling on your own, it's best to ask for time to consider a written offer in privacy. A day or two is not unreasonable and will give you a chance to consult your attorney and formulate a written response.

If you use an agent, you will probably hear first by telephone that a written offer has come in on your property. Because offers must be presented immediately, you might even be notified while you are out of town.

Most homeowners react by asking immediately how much the buyer is prepared to pay. The agent, however, will usually parry such questions. Revealing the purchase price over the telephone, without discussing accompanying matters, is considered a poor practice. You will probably be asked to set a time for face-to-face presentation of the offer. Some brokers ask a secretary to set up the appointment, heading off your direct request for information. You will be asked to name a time when all owners of the property can be present.

When you have listed your home with one member of a Multiple Listing Service and the offer is secured by another office, local custom governs the procedure. The offer may be turned over to your listing agent for presentation. In other areas, the selling office may contact you directly. Or your lister may be notified and asked to set up the appointment for the selling broker. In any event, you may request that your original agent attend the meeting for presentation of the offer. The buyer will probably not be present.

154. What will happen if there's more than one offer?

Bear in mind that your agent, although duty-bound to find you the best deal, is naturally eager to sell the home through his or her own office and thus retain the whole commission. When an offer comes in, double-check: ask whether any other offers are in preparation elsewhere or rumored to be in the offing.

If several offers come in, it is best to consider all of them at the same time. The one first signed by a would-be buyer does not have precedence. As long as you have not acted on any offer, you are free to consider all of them and to respond to whichever one you choose.

In some areas, notably around New York City, the broker brings you a simple memorandum of price and terms for the proposed purchase. In other areas, the purchase offer is a detailed proposal. If you sign an acceptance, it becomes a full-fledged, binding purchase contract.

Throughout the country, brokers believe one transaction in ten goes through at list price; the proportion may well be different in your area. Among factors that could limit the price offered are the cost of comparable properties now on the market, the buyer's knowledge of recent similar sales and—often most important—the buyer's ability to pay. Bear in mind that although you and the buyers can agree on any price, there may be problems ahead if they cannot carry a proposed mortgage loan or if the lender makes an unfavorable appraisal of your home's value.

155. What terms can I expect to see in the offer?

The buyers will detail the terms on which they plan to buy the property. Before you take your home off the market on their behalf, you want some assurance that the transaction is likely to conclude successfully.

If you receive an all-cash offer, ask the broker, their attorney or the buyers themselves about their ability to come up with that amount of money and the source of the funds. Although this might appear to be none of your business, you will be making a decision based on their ability to fulfill their obligations.

If the buyer wants to take over your present mortgage, your lawyer can advise you of any legal complications. Ask for an explanation of contingent liability; with some mortgages, particularly when your buyer does not submit qualification information to the lender, you will retain liability for the loan even after you sell the property.

If the buyer plans to place a new loan on the property, you may be asked to pay points to a lending institution. This subject is discussed at length in Chapter 21.

You may be asked to take back the financing—that is, hold the mortgage yourself. Before agreeing to such an arrangement, read carefully the section on purchase money mortgages in Chapter 21. You can make your response conditional: "I accept the offer, subject to verification of buyer's employment and income and a satisfactory credit report."

156. What are contingencies?

Often, the buyers will make their offer subject to certain happenings or contingencies. This means they promise to buy the property but:

- only if they are able to secure an FHA mortgage loan in the amount of $92,000 with interest at a certain percent;
- only if they sell their present home;
- only if a spouse approves the new home; or
- only if there is a satisfactory engineering report.

Other contingencies are possible. To protect yourself, each contingency should be accompanied by a time limit. The engineer's report can usually be obtained within three days; so might the spouse's approval. You will not run much of a risk if you accept and take your home off the market for a few days.

The stipulation that financing must be obtained is understandable. You can request that the buyer promise prompt application to a lending institution. The contract may even stipulate that the buyer will apply to three lending institutions, if necessary, and under the guidance of your agent. Again, a time limit can be set for application and, as with all the provisions of the agreement, everything must be in writing within the contract itself.

Whether you should accept an offer contingent on the sale of the buyer's home depends on your situation and how urgent is your need to sell.

When the contingency is for the sale of the buyer's present property, use your best judgment. Some sellers simply refuse all contingent offers. Others find them reasonable because buyers may need money from their sale to buy another house.

When you accept an offer contingent on the sale of the buyer's present home, you trade worry about the sale of your own property for worry about the sale of someone else's, over which you have no control. You have a right to investigate how likely the other house is to sell and whether it is being listed at a reasonable price. You can even insert into your contract provisions about this matter.

The terms of an offer—whether it is a clean, all-cash deal or one that involves a contingency—often affect the sale price eventually agreed upon. If you are going to wait for the sale of the buyer's house, you have some justification for sticking to a higher price in return for the uncertainty.

Make sure that any offer contingent upon the sale of the buyer's present property includes an escape clause, sometimes called a kick-out. This provision allows you to continue showing your home. If you receive another offer that you want to accept, you notify the first buyers that they must remove their contingency or withdraw. Either they agree to buy your home by the specified date, come what may, or they must void the contract and drop out of the picture, allowing you to negotiate with your new purchaser.

Local custom suggests the exact terms of the escape clause. You might allow a period of one month in which the buyers can be secure in their contract; after that, if their own home hasn't sold, they could be bumped by another offer. Usually, you promise the first buyers a period of three to five business days in which to make their decision should an escape clause be invoked.

The problem is, though, that once your home is sold on a contingent basis, most brokers won't continue showing it.

The purchase contract should detail all of the gray-area items mentioned at the time of listing: swing sets, carpeting, mirrors, chandeliers and, in general, all fixtures that you will leave with the property. In addition, you may agree to include items of personal property such as kitchen appliances, washer and dryer or drapes.

The contract should also mention those items you will remove. Oral agreement is not a sufficient guarantee against misunderstandings later.

157. How much earnest money is necessary to make a contract binding?

None.

The deposit is not a legal requirement for the contract. If the cash for the purchase must come from the sale of the buyer's present home, the buyer may be unable to deposit earnest money or may be reluctant to do so. You should not accept an offer, however, unless it is accompanied by some sort of deposit. The money signifies that the buyer means business.

Your buyers are asked to put a deposit into the hands of the broker to prove that their intentions are serious and to serve as a source of damages should they back out for no good reason. You can expect to see their safeguards written into the contract: that their deposit will be returned if the lender's appraisal comes in below the purchase price, if you renege for no good reason or if they fail to receive their mortgage commitment, for example. You can request a similar provision: that the deposit is in jeopardy if they do not act in good faith.

158. What should I watch out for concerning the deposit?

Local custom varies, and the buyers may have been told that 1, 2, 6 or even 10 percent is standard. They may well come up with less. One thousand dollars is a respectable deposit, and even a smaller sum may suffice to make the buyers feel a commitment to going through with the transaction.

In some areas, it's customary for buyers to make a smaller deposit at the time they sign the offer, with the contract stating that they will increase the deposit by a specific amount when the offer is accepted.

Pay attention to the form of the deposit. The buyers may be out-of-towners who do not keep large sums in a checking account; have they promised to make the check good as soon as they get back home? A promissory note is of little value in this matter, and a cash deposit of $500 is often more useful than a note for $5,000.

The broker is legally liable to you for any representation about the earnest money because you base your decisions on what you are told. Insist that you be notified immediately when the deposit check clears, when a note or post-dated check is made good and—particularly important—if there is any holdup in the process.

Buyers may be understandably reluctant to hand a deposit directly to you, the seller. If an agent is involved, the money is usually kept in the broker's escrow account. If there is no agent, explain that the money will be held by your attorney or, failing that, by the buyers' attorney or an escrow company.

159. What else goes in the contract?

The purchase contract will contain details on those items that must be apportioned between you and the buyer at closing: water bills, property taxes and the like. It stipulates the type of deed you must deliver, which party bears responsibility for loss resulting from fire before the time of closing, the procedure if a cloud on the title is found and many other matters intended to head off disagreements as the transaction progresses. A closing date will be specified. Unless the powerful legal clause "time being of the essence" is included, the closing date mentioned is merely a target and might come and go with the contract still continuing in effect. If a certain date is essential to you, be sure to consult your lawyer before declaring time of the essence.

Possession of the property is usually given on the date of settlement. It rarely becomes necessary to let the buyers move in ahead of time or for you to remain after closing. If the buyer moves in as a tenant, take certain precautions (discussed in Chapter 22); try to avoid such an arrangement. Many brokers and lawyers say bluntly that you should *never* let the buyer move in before closing.

If you plan to stay on after closing, you may be asked to pay rent and even to deposit a large sum in escrow to ensure that you will eventually move out as agreed. Like all other arrangements, this should be written into the original sales contract.

To safeguard yourself, you may wish to include certain limitations in the contract. Perhaps you will make repairs, if they are required by the lending institution, only up to a certain dollar amount. You may want to limit the number of points you pay. If appliances are included in the sale, you will want to transfer them "as is" where state law permits.

The offer you receive will probably contain a time limit— "This offer is good until Saturday noon." In most states, the buyers are free to withdraw their offer until you have accepted it. If they do not, and if you accept before Saturday noon, you have a firm purchase contract, binding upon both parties.

160. Are "yes" and "no" the only possible responses to an offer?

Not at all. There's also "maybe."

"Yes" is an acceptance of the offer as it stands, without any alteration. You can write above your signature the words *subject to the approval of my attorney*. In this case, your lawyer must later approve the wording and provisions of the contract. If he or she does not, you may void the contract, or both parties may agree to amend it. In some states, your lawyer automatically has this right for a certain number of days, and so does the buyers' attorney.

You may have arranged beforehand to telephone your lawyer while you consider the purchase offer. Some attorneys do not mind holding themselves available during the out-of-office hours that may be involved. If the offer is on a standard form with which the lawyer is familiar, a few minutes may suffice to go over the specific terms detailed so that you can receive legal counsel by phone.

Alternatively, you can take the contract to your lawyer before you accept it. Keep two precautions in mind, however. First, many attorneys will not counsel you on price, a matter that they consider out of their field of expertise. And second, there is always the possibility that you have a nit-picking lawyer, unaccustomed to real estate transactions, who may delay and fuss around until you lose a favorable offer. In the end, you must make your own decision, taking into account the advice of both agent and attorney.

Then there's "no."

You can always refuse an offer completely. Once you have rejected it, you cannot change your mind, even five minutes later, and get it back. Suppose, for example, that the offer is good until Saturday at noon. On Friday night, you reject it. You cannot then change your mind on Saturday morning and accept it. If you wanted to, you would have to ask the buyers whether they would reinstate their offer.

Because you know that an underpriced house sells quickly, you may be skeptical of a good offer that comes in promptly. It is only human to argue that, "If I received an offer for $120,000 after only one week, what might I get by waiting a while longer?" The true bargain, however, is usually snapped up within a day or two. After a week, you can assume the market is operating normally. Experience has shown that the first offer is often the best one. This is because a new home on the market is exposed to a large group of potential buyers. Your best offer is likely to come from that group. Be cautious, then, about rejecting a first offer out of hand. An agent finds little comfort in saying "I told you so" if you are still waiting vainly three months later for a proposal to equal the first one.

161. So what's a "maybe" response?

Better than a simple refusal is a counteroffer. With a counter-offer, you agree to accept the buyers' proposal if a few changes are made.

Again, you run the risk of losing your buyers. You have not accepted their proposal, and they are now free to accept or reject yours. At least, though, a counteroffer, with its possibility for reaching eventual agreement, is better than an outright rejection.

While a counteroffer is pending, your home is more or less tied up. Therefore, make the counteroffer good for only a short period of time, perhaps a day or two.

If your home has turned out to be a hot property and you anticipate other offers within the next few days, you may prefer not to be bound by a written counteroffer. "Tell the buyer to come back $5,000 higher and I'll consider it," you might say informally to the agent, without committing yourself.

Inexperienced negotiators sometimes assume that the proper procedure is for the buyer to start with a low offer and for the seller to counter somewhat under the asking price, depending on a series of counter-counteroffers to bring them eventually to a price halfway between. In practice, too many counters usually kill a transaction. The parties lose sight of the main goal—reaching an agreement—as emotions rise and the process becomes a test of wills.

Your buyers are well advised to make their first offer as high as they are prepared to go, and you should make any counter-offer close to the price you would really take. If you are determined to stand pat on your list price, consider the buyers' pride and offer a token reduction—perhaps a few hundred dollars—to signal your goodwill. Offer to throw in the refriger-ator or the drapes. These could be items that the buyers do not particularly want, but they provide a way for the buyer to save face while accepting your price. At least, they may reason, their low offer was not wasted, for it won some concessions.

During price negotiations, it is essential to remember your objective. You may insist on the last few dollars as a matter of principle, completely overlooking the fact that when you set your original asking price, that extra thousand was tacked on "just to see."

A counteroffer may concern itself with matters other than price. You might "accept all terms and conditions except that purchase price shall be $132,000," or "accept all terms and conditions except that date of closing shall be June 30th." Or you might request that an escape clause be added to the contingency regarding the sale of the buyers' present property. Any of the terms discussed earlier in this chapter can be added to your counteroffer. Special circumstances may suggest other provisions. As long as both parties agree and the matter is not illegal, almost anything can be written into your contract. For unusual provisions, wording should be supplied by your attorney or the buyers'.

162. Who signs the sales contract?

When you and the buyers have signed an exact acceptance of all terms, the contract is binding and the commission has theoretically been earned.

It is not essential for all buyers to sign the offer, but all sellers must. In some states, various provisions dictate that a spouse sign, even if not an owner of record.

Chapter 21

*U*nderstanding Why Your Buyer's Financing Is Your Business

*Y*ou may think financing is the buyer's concern, but it is of vital importance to you. How will you respond to these questions?

"Are you willing to consider an FHA offer?"

"Will you hold the mortgage yourself for high interest and a five-year balloon?"

"Can I take over your VA loan if I'm not a veteran?"

"Would you drop your price $15,000 for all cash?"

Preparing to judge the buyer's financing proposal requires homework on your part. Become familiar with the possibilities. Ask an agent for a briefing on the current alternatives. Find out about new and innovative programs as they become available locally.

There is no single best financing plan out there. More than a hundred mortgage plans are available from lending institutions in almost any locality. Each of these plans fits a certain situation best—buyer's need, seller's convenience, type of property.

To ask, "What's the best mortgage around right now?" is like walking into a shoe store and asking, "What's the best pair of shoes you have?" The answer depends, of course—are you going hiking? Dancing? Wearing brown or black? Do you have big feet or small? Are you a man or a woman?

A broker, working with a buyer, develops a financing strategy for that buyer within the first few minutes of conversation. Recent bankrupt? Better search for an assumable mortgage. Two young professionals? Suggest an ARM. Ambitious young carpenter? Find an older seller with a run-down house that can't be financed through a regular lender.

163. How do I find out about the buyer's finances?

If you are using a real estate broker, your agent will "qualify" the buyer. The process involves an analysis of income, debts, assets, credit rating and available cash, to determine whether the buyer is financially capable of purchasing your home.

If the buyers have retained their own buyer's broker, that financial information is confidential, but you are entitled to an honest answer to "Do you consider the buyer well qualified financially to purchase my property?" and you are also entitled to disclosure of the buyer's financial inability or unwillingness to complete the transaction. That disclosure should come whether or not you know enough to ask for it, just as *your* agent must disclose any hidden defect about your property to customers.

If you are selling on your own, you need some assurance about the buyer's financial situation before you accept an offer and take your home off the market. The buyer who is serious should not mind filling out a financial statement that you can take to your lawyer or accountant for analysis before you make a firm commitment to sell. One of a seller's worst mistakes is tying up the house for months, only to find that the prospective buyer is financially unable to complete the purchase.

You can ask—and this is true whether you sell on your own or not—that the would-be buyers bring you a written prequalifying commitment from a lending institution. They should be able to secure such a document within a few days. You can ask to see it before you sign an acceptance of their offer, or you can sign an acceptance of the contract subject to their producing it.

164. Should I hold out for all cash?

Most agents can count on one hand the number of contracts they have written involving all-cash purchases. Such buyers are so few that the subject is easily disposed of. The advantages to you in an all-cash sale are these:

- You will not be asked to pay points to a lender.
- You will receive your money immediately.
- The closing date may be set for your convenience because no mortgage commitment need be obtained.
- With no contingencies for obtaining financing, you can count on a firm sale and make your plans with confidence.

Possible negatives are these:

- You may prefer not to receive all proceeds immediately, for income tax or personal reasons.
- The buyer, aware of the value of an all-cash sale, may expect a price concession in return. (Consider giving it!)

Before accepting an all-cash offer, though, insist on proof that the money is available (a "gift letter" from a grandmother isn't really proof—are you sure she has the money?). Insist upon a substantial deposit, with a written provision that it will be forfeited if the buyer is unable to perform.

165. What should I do if the buyer wants to assume my loan?

Your mortgage may or may not be assumable by the next owner of the house. If it is, it will fall into one of two categories: freely assumable or assumable with lender's approval.

Freely assumable mortgages include all FHA loans placed before December 1, 1986, and all VA loans placed before March 1, 1988. (More about new rules for FHA and VA loans placed after those dates in a moment.) If your mortgage is one of these, any buyer may take it, along with the house, with no change in interest rate or term.

The buyers need not prove that they can qualify to carry the loan. The lending institution has no say in the matter. All that is necessary is your assent. The buyers pay the difference in cash at time of closing, or they may request that you hold a second mortgage—more on that later. Suppose, for example, that you own a $100,000 home with a VA loan on which you presently owe $85,000. The buyer (who need not be a veteran) can take the loan along with the house, paying you the remaining $15,000 in cash.

166. What are the advantages if my loan is freely assumable?

- As with an all-cash sale, no points are due, you receive your money immediately, the sale is firm and the closing date need not be subject to a lender's convenience.
- Your home should be easily sold because many buyers look for such mortgages and can afford the down payments. Your loan, which may have a lower interest rate than is currently available, may be the most valuable thing about your home.

• You may command a premium for your property. The fortunate buyer has few closing costs to pay, saves on mortgage or appraisal fees and need not pass bank inspection. The buyer may be willing to pay something extra for the savings anticipated over the years from a low-interest rate.

167. Are there drawbacks to allowing takeover of a freely assumable mortgage?

Think carefully before allowing an assumption if the buyer wants you to take back a second mortgage for most or all of the remaining purchase price. Observe the procedures listed under Question 174 later in this chapter. It is particularly risky if the buyers have no cash of their own in the property; the buyers would have little to lose if things got bad and they just left the key in the mailbox and walked away.

Perhaps the major drawback to allowing this type of mortgage assumption is that you retain contingent liability. If the mortgage were foreclosed and the property could not be sold for enough money to clear the debt, the lender, FHA or VA could require you to make up the deficiency. This possibility becomes more remote with every passing day, however, as the debt is reduced and if the dollar value of the home increases. Caution is indicated, though, in a neighborhood that is deteriorating or an area that is economically depressed.

There is a procedure under which the new borrower, if willing, can prove qualifications and release the seller from further liability. The buyer who assumes an older VA loan, if the seller is to be released, must be a veteran with an entitlement.

168. What if my mortgage is assumable with approval?

For FHA loans made after December 15, 1989, and VA mortgages placed after March 1, 1988, the buyer assuming the loan must prove financial qualification to the satisfaction of the lending institution. The original borrower would have no further liability.

If the buyer assuming this newer FHA loan is not able or willing to prove qualification, a simple credit check and appraisal of the property may be substituted, and the seller retains liability for five years. After that time, if mortgage payments are current, the original borrower is no longer liable.

Conventional loans, those not backed by the FHA or VA, are usually not freely assumable. The majority must be paid off when the property is sold. But some are assumable with the lender's approval. Many adjustable-rate mortgages (ARMs) fall into this group.

If your present mortgage is of this type, your buyer can apply to the lender to assume your loan. The new borrower must prove qualification to carry the debt and, in the case of an ARM, the interest rate may be adjusted. Closing costs are less than those required for placing a new loan.

Conventional mortgages vary in this matter and in other provisions. If yours is being assumed, your attorney can tell you whether you run any risks.

169. What should I do if my home is unique and won't meet bank standards?

When every lender in town sets the same limits on some of their loans, and the same guidelines on the property involved, chances are the regulations are set by the secondary mortgage market. Many lenders make loans, then turn around and sell them (packaged with many other mortgages) to big investors in the secondary mortgage market. The largest buyer in this field is Fannie Mae, the Federal National Mortgage Association. When Fannie Mae announces that it will buy a certain type of mortgage, lending institutions listen.

If you or the buyer has a situation that doesn't meet the standards of the secondary market, search for a local lender making *portfolio loans*. These are old-fashioned mortgages in which the bank (or savings and loan institution) lends its own money, collects and keeps the payments and retains the mortgages in its own portfolio. Because such loans don't have to meet the nationwide standards of the secondary market, lenders can be more flexible. The buyer of an antique house that doesn't meet current building standards or a self-employed buyer with unusual qualifications might well need a portfolio loan.

170. Why should I pay points on the buyer's mortgage?

The payment of points when a new mortgage loan is made compensates the lender for an interest rate that does not reflect the true cost of the money. Each point is 1 percent of the loan being placed. It is due as a one-time, lump-sum payment, usually at the time of transfer of title.

If your buyer is looking for a $100,000 mortgage, for example, and the lending institution demands four points, $4,000 will be due.

When interest rates fluctuate daily, lending institutions prefer to change the number of points charged rather than constantly alter the interest rates on mortgages. The number of points charged thus may vary from one lender to another and from one week to another. Keeping track of the local situation is one of a broker's major concerns.

If $4,000 is due in points before your buyer can place a $100,000 mortgage, who pays this sum? The answer depends on what is negotiated in your sales contract. If you are committed to paying points, make sure the buyers consider your interests when they choose a lender.

In times of high interest rates, which might make it impossible for your buyer to qualify for the proposed mortgage loan, you may be asked to participate in a buydown—a relatively new idea. A lending institution offers you the opportunity to pay extra points; in return, your buyers can place their loan at a lower interest rate. Although this process reduces your proceeds from the home, it does enable the buyers to purchase.

Although points represent up-front interest payments, they are subject to varying treatment by the Internal Revenue Service. The buyer of your home can deduct immediately, in the year they are paid, all points (even those you pay) on a mortgage to buy a residence.

Most important to you, points paid by the seller are merely a cost of selling. They may reduce your capital gain, but if you're using one of the special homesellers' tax breaks (see Chapter 24), that may not save you any money.

This factor may be significant when you work out a sales contract; points (if the buyer has the extra money to pay them) don't cost the buyer as much as they cost you because they represent an income tax deduction for the buyer.

171. What are conventional mortgages?

Conventional loans are those transactions negotiated between borrower and lender with no government backing— regular bank mortgages. If the buyer puts down less than 10 or 20 percent, a conventional loan may require the borrower to purchase private mortgage insurance (PMI) to protect the lender in case of default.

Your advantages, if the buyer secures a conventional loan, include the following:

- The application process can be less complicated than it is with an FHA or a VA loan, and the time between application and mortgage commitment is sometimes shorter.
- The lender is more concerned with the security of the loan than with the condition of the house, so you are less likely to be asked to make repairs than with FHA- or VA-backed mortgages.

Drawbacks to conventional loans, from your point of view, are these:

- They usually involve large down payments unless PMI is purchased. In a difficult mortgage market, down payment requirements and interest rates may rise to impractically high levels, effectively shutting out many of your potential buyers.
- A bank will base its loan on the value reported by its own appraiser.

You don't need to learn much about adjustable-rate mortgages. Whether to choose one or not is usually the buyer's decision, and it doesn't affect you.

172. Should I accept an offer if the buyer is looking for an FHA or VA mortgage?

These loans, government insured or guaranteed, are oriented to the borrower's benefit. Because the money comes from local lenders, they may not be available in all localities, and the top loan amount, particularly in the case of FHA, is of limited use for higher priced homes.

A number of special FHA programs are available with little or no down payment. VA loans can be made with no down payment.

If your home falls within the price limits for these loans, you will have a wide pool of buyers. The low down payment provisions, as well as the fact that all of these mortgages are assumable with lender's approval if the house is later resold, make FHA and VA loans attractive to buyers.

A stringent inspection of the property is conducted, and specific repairs may be requested before the mortgage is granted. In most cases, repairs must be paid for by the seller. You always have the option, though, of refusing to make repairs and voiding the contract. Your contract can state that you will make repairs only up to a given dollar amount.

If you have a solid buyer who is short of cash, both the FHA and VA will allow you to pay some of the buyer's closing costs. Indeed, the VA will even allow a generous seller to pay all the buyer's costs, prepaid taxes, points, the works. With VA mortgages requiring no down payment, a lucky veteran could theoretically get in with no cash outlay at all. Why would a seller agree to such an arrangement?

To get the home sold.

173. What are Farmers Home loans?

In some rural areas, the Rural Economic and Community Development Administration (formerly the Farmers Home Administration), a division of the U.S. Department of Agriculture, makes direct loans to buyers. Strict income limits are set, usually in low-income to middle-income brackets, and monthly payments are tailored to a borrower's income. You might find a buyer who plans to use the FmHA if you are located in an area with fewer than 10,000 residents and your home is of modest size and price. One drawback is that the source of loans can be cut off when available funds are depleted for the fiscal quarter-year. An advantage, though, is that the FmHA qualifies and approves borrowers before they've even found homes to buy.

174. Should I consider taking back a mortgage?

Although any loan used for buying real estate is strictly called a *purchase-money mortgage,* the term is often employed for seller financing, those transactions in which you are asked to "take back" the loan yourself. These arrangements are possible, of course, only when you do not need your proceeds immediately for the purchase of another home.

You may lend money on a first mortgage, the buyer's primary loan on the property. Or you may take back a second mortgage, lending the buyer some of the down payment needed to assume your first mortgage.

When times get rough in the mortgage market, you may receive proposals for *creative financing,* a term that denotes all sorts of ingenious devices for making a detour around regular mortgage arrangements.

One possibility is a land contract, or contract for deed. With this arrangement, you retain title to the property until the buyer has made all the payments to you. Or a land contract may be in effect only until the buyer has paid enough to constitute an acceptable down payment, at which time you turn over title (give the buyer a deed).

Often, a purchase-money mortgage involves a balloon arrangement. You may not be willing to wait 30 years for your money, yet the buyer cannot afford the large monthly payments necessary to retire the debt in five years. Payments are, therefore, set as if the mortgage were indeed for a 30-year period. At the end of five years, however, the entire remaining debt becomes due and payable; that large lump-sum payment is the balloon. The understanding is that either you will renew the loan or the buyer will be able, by that time, to arrange outside financing. With the average family moving every five years, the house may have changed hands and the debt may have been paid off anyway.

175. What are the advantages to seller financing?

If you can afford to wait for your money, the advantages to yourself are as follows:

- Your house is more easily sold in a difficult mortgage period.
- You may have income tax advantages if you receive your money over a period of years.
- You may be able to hold out for a higher sales price because you are doing the buyer a favor.
- A house that cannot pass a lender's inspection can be sold this way with fewer complications.
- You will not owe points to a lender.

176. Are there drawbacks to seller financing?

There is really only one disadvantage, but it's a big one.

Will the buyers meet their responsibilities, or will you find yourself with the house—and a host of problems—back on your hands?

If you consider taking back financing, a number of precautions are in order.

First, make sure that you receive a down payment large enough to cover the expenses of selling, the ready cash you need from the property and as much more as possible. A large down payment represents safety for you because it means that should you ever have to foreclose, the debt may be covered by the sale of the property. A large down payment also serves to separate strong buyers from weak ones.

Next, insist on an analysis of the borrowers' financial position in much the same way a regular lending institution would. Your lawyer or broker can obtain a credit report on the buyers, and it is essential that it be satisfactory, indicating that they meet their financial obligations on time. Any compromise on this point is unwise.

It's often buyers who cannot meet bank standards who ask you to take back financing. You have to ask yourself: am I ready to take a chance on them when a regular lender won't? In such a case, it's not much use requesting that they secure a prequalifying bank commitment because obviously they can't. You can certainly ask the same questions a lender would, though.

Analyze the buyers' present debts and income to ensure that they are not getting in over their heads. Look for job stability and prospects of advancement.

177. What if the buyer wants me to hold a second mortgage?

You may be asked to lend the buyer some of the money needed to assume your present loan. Second mortgages usually carry higher interest rates than first mortgages. Later, if you prefer your money in one lump sum, you can sell the second mortgage at a discount to an investor. The large discount may surprise you, though, even if payments are being made as promised.

The second mortgage carries a higher degree of risk than a first. In case of foreclosure, the property would be sold and the proceeds used to pay off unpaid taxes and the first mortgage before you receive payment on your second mortgage. There might not be sufficient funds, in that case, to cover your loan. Again, your best protection is a large down payment.

178. Is a lease option a good way to sell?

A lease option commits you to sell the property for a given amount of money at any time within a stated term. (Other provisions may apply.) Your tenants/purchasers are usually free to buy or not to buy. If they decide not to exercise their option to purchase, they commonly remain on the property as simple tenants and may forfeit the money they put up in a lump-sum payment for the option.

From the seller's point of view, a lease option can be a fine device for securing good tenants who will take care of the property as if it were their own. The arrangement may, however, result in no sale at all—or a forced sale you didn't really want.

179. How much will a buyer need in income to buy my home?

If you are selling on your own, it is wise to determine, at the start, how much income a buyer will need to qualify for your home. How much buyers will need to borrow, of course, depends on how much they can put down. There's no way you can guess the amount of cash your eventual buyer will have on hand, but it's safe to say that most buyers borrow as much as possible. Loans commonly run from 80 percent to, in the case of a VA loan, 100 percent of the value of a home.

As a rule of thumb, consider that a buyer will need annual income of at least two-fifths of your selling price. If your home is worth $200,000, they'd need income of at least $80,000 a year. Every borrower's situation is different, of course. More or less cash available for a down payment makes a difference, and so does their other indebtedness. If they have substantial car loans, revolving credit accounts or student loans, they'll probably need more income to qualify. On the other hand, if your property taxes are relatively low, they might need a bit less.

Chapter 22

*W*aiting for Your Closing Day

*W*hen can you joyfully spread the news of the sale to your friends? Is it the day someone first expresses an intention to buy? The time when you reach written agreement on price and terms? Or the final settlement session, when the money and the front-door key change hands?

Although most transactions do proceed smoothly from contract to eventual transfer of title, you, the agent and the buyer all have responsibilities while the sale is "in the tunnel." All of you can help ensure the successful outcome of your mutual plans.

Your agent or lawyer will furnish duplicate originals of the final purchase agreement, which has now become a binding contract, to you, the buyer, the lending institution, the escrow agent or other parties involved.

Depending on closing customs in your area, you may be asked to furnish copies of your deed, survey, last paid tax bill or abstract.

When a new mortgage is being placed, the agent should assist in selecting the most favorable lending institution and may accompany the borrower to the application interview. If no agent is involved, check to see that prompt application is being made.

Unless you already know that the deposit is safely tucked into an escrow account, you are entitled to a report on its progress. If you are not notified when the check clears or the promissory note is made good, do not hesitate to inquire.

Merely finding a buyer for the property will not ensure a successful sale. You, your lawyer or your agent must ride herd on the mortgage application process. You want to hear as soon as possible that the buyers' credit checked out well and the house appraised at a satisfactory figure.

Or you may hear about holdups in the paperwork: the verification of employment form has not been returned or a required inspection has not been documented. It may be necessary to arrange appointments for an appraiser, an inspecting engineer, a termite inspector or a surveyor.

180. What should I say to the buyer before closing?

Say as little as possible. Just be friendly.

Remember that buyers often are jittery, worrying about whether they made the right decision. A malady known as Buyers' Remorse can set in during this period, often at 2:00 AM. You also face change and upheaval and probably are not quite yourself. It may be advisable to talk with the buyers through your broker or lawyer. Any contact you do have should be cordial and reassuring but also limited and noncommittal. Many queries are best answered, "I'm not sure; I'm leaving that to my lawyer," or "The broker probably knows about it."

The buyers may have seen your house for half an hour at most on only one occasion. It is understandable if they desire a closer inspection. They may want to measure for curtains, show the place to parents or take some pictures. If there is a broker, he or she should accompany them to handle sudden doubts that may arise. Of course you have a binding contract, but the sale will go more smoothly with buyers who are eager to complete the transaction.

At this point, you may want to let the buyers know which appliances or furniture you will be selling. Keep your negotiations friendly, and remember that you can always advertise a garage sale for whatever is left.

If you are not using an agent, keep in touch with the buyers about the progress of the mortgage application. Your lawyer, familiar with the lender's requirements, can also check on the process, but of course it's less expensive to do it yourself.

181. What should I do if the buyer needs to move in before closing?

Don't let it happen.

Brokers and lawyers agree that it is a poor idea to allow the buyer to move in before closing. If circumstances dictate such an arrangement, discuss the matter thoroughly with your attorney. Among points to be considered in a moving-in agreement are these:

- The buyer must first have passed the bank's credit check.
- A high security deposit must be established. Some sellers require that all of the cash the buyer will need at closing be deposited.
- The buyers promise not to make any changes in the property until they own it.
- Rent might be set at a higher rate than the prospective mortgage payments so that there will be an incentive to go to settlement on time.
- A written agreement should promise that the buyers will accept everything "as is" on the day they move in. Who pays for subsequent repairs should be settled in advance.
- Insurance liability must be checked.
- Your accountant can advise whether the rental period jeopardizes your special tax treatment for profit on the sale of your own home.

Try to avoid letting the buyers in before closing if it's at all possible. It's easy, if they have second thoughts, to find all sorts of small objections to the house and hold up or even frustrate the closing. And if they don't receive the mortgage commitment or something holds up the closing, it might be difficult to evict them.

If the house is vacant and the buyers want to come in to measure for curtains, that's understandable. But if they want to paint some rooms, rip out the kitchen cabinets or get a head start on refinishing the floors, think twice about letting them. There's many a slip twixt the cup and the lip, and if the place doesn't close as promised, you could be left with a mess.

182. What should the buyer do to prepare for closing?

Your buyer must act in good faith to fulfill any conditions stipulated in the purchase contract. If a new loan is being sought, the buyer must make application promptly at a lending institution appropriate to the financing planned and must cooperate in securing the necessary papers.

If the purchasers must sell their present home, you may have specified in the contract that they will list it immediately in the open market. Seldom will you have control, however, over the price they ask for the property or how they answer purchase offers they receive.

The contract will contain your agreements concerning which party will arrange and pay for termite inspection, survey, an engineer's report and such matters. Usually these responsibilities are established by community custom. During the waiting period, brokers, buyer or seller, their attorneys or the escrow agent will attend to these items.

Flood insurance, if required by the lender, must be purchased by the buyer. The buyers will be asked by the lender to prove that they are placing adequate hazard insurance on the property. They must arrange this before closing.

The buyers will be notified just before closing about how much cash they will need; then they should obtain a certified or cashier's check for that amount.

183. What problems could come up for me before closing?

You may be informed, to your surprise, that the roofer with whom you quarreled last fall has filed a mechanic's lien that encumbers your title to the house. To clear this lien, pay it off. Your lawyer may be willing to convey the good news to the contractor; the worker may be so delighted at the prospect of payment that a compromise sum is agreed upon. If you prefer to challenge the lien, you can release it by posting a bond pending adjudication.

Other liens against your house must be cleared (unpaid taxes, personal judgments).

A title search may disclose unexpected claims against the property by your former spouse or by long-ago heirs of a previous owner. A simple quitclaim deed may be used in such cases. By signing this deed, the person involved waives any rights he or she might have, without laying claim to the property.

If you are caught between two homes and won't receive the proceeds from the old one in time to close on the new, a specific type of short-term loan is possible. Banks call such a loan interim financing, a swing loan, a bridging loan or a turnaround. Your attorney or broker can help you investigate this.

If at the closing you will pay off a mortgage held by a regular lending institution, you'll receive an exact payoff figure for the date of closing. If you will pay off a mortgage held by a private individual (perhaps the person from whom you bought the property), special precautions are in order. You are entitled to receive a certificate of satisfaction stating that the loan has been paid off; in some states, this is a reconveyance deed.

This document is of great importance, as it will be entered in the public records to give the world notice that your debt is paid off. While lending institutions are used to furnishing the document, a private lender may not be. Your attorney, or the person in charge of the closing, should secure the certificate, signed by the lender, and hold it until your payoff is made.

If the buyer will pay all cash and no new mortgage will be recorded, it's still important to secure that certificate.

184. Will I have to make repairs to my property?

That depends on the condition of the house, the type of mortgage loan being sought and the written promises you made when you accepted the purchase offer.

If a new mortgage loan is being sought, two hurdles must be cleared before title to a house can be transferred. The house must be appraised at the agreed-upon sales price, and it must meet the lender's standards for condition.

In some areas, particularly if the house is a multiple dwelling, repairs may be required before transfer of title. When a new FHA or VA loan is being placed, the buyer pays for an appraisal and inspection. The report may stipulate specific repairs needed before the mortgage can be placed. The FHA standards deal primarily with the health and safety of the occupants and preservation of the structure. If your exterior paint is shabby, it need not be redone. If, however, bare wood is evident, a paint job will be required to preserve the material. Redecorating will not be required on the interior, but a handrail for the basement steps might be requested.

You are not bound to make these repairs unless specified in your contract. If you choose not to, you may void the contract and start looking for another buyer. This means, of course, that you are back to square one, with the additional handicap of not wanting to consider any further FHA or VA offers.

It is usually better to proceed with the repairs specified. With certain programs, the buyer may volunteer to assist; with others, you must do the work yourself. If you cannot afford the repairs, ask your broker's help in finding a worker who will wait until the day of transfer for payment.

If the work can't be done—exterior paint, for example, with closing set for a northern winter day—you can sometimes agree to have part of the purchase price held in escrow, to be released after closing when the work is completed.

185. Suppose the house "doesn't appraise"?

If the lender's appraiser doesn't find the house worth at least the amount of the sale price, the lending institution will refuse to base its loan on that price. With FHA or VA contracts, your buyer has the option of dropping out at this point, and depending on the wording of the contract, other buyers may have the same right.

Buyers may be so upset by the notification that they will quit. Often, though, the problem is solved by renegotiation. You might drop your price to the amount of the appraisal, or the buyers might agree to make a larger down payment. Often, a compromise is worked out, with each party giving up something.

If your purchasers plan to obtain a new mortgage loan, the progress of their application is of great importance. You can expect the broker to monitor the process, and the attorney for either party may also check up from time to time.

The application process consists mainly of assembling exhibits, various documents that will affect the lender's decision. One exhibit is the credit history of the buyers.

The buyers' income will be verified by their employers. On the rare occasion when cooperation is not forthcoming, payroll stubs or income tax returns will be brought in by the applicant instead.

An unpleasant surprise may turn up at this point. Forgotten or unknown judgments against the buyers may surface, even as they might in your own records. These are not fatal to the application. The buyer can clear them by paying them off.

More serious is the discovery that the prospective purchasers have been less than frank about their credit history. A bankruptcy they "forgot" to mention, or several large debts presently outstanding, can seriously threaten their chances for the loan.

If such problems develop, you have a right to be notified immediately, for time is money in your situation. If there is a chance that the transaction might fall through, you should be told at once. Your lawyer or broker can assess the possibility of failure.

You can always put your house back on the market, subject to nonperformance of the existing contract. This enables you to start searching for another buyer immediately, pending the outcome of the present problem. It is, of course, a serious step and should be considered only when the outlook becomes dark.

186. What should I do if the whole thing blows up?

If your transaction falls apart, your lawyer's help will be essential in advising you of your rights or responsibilities. Should you back out for no legally acceptable reason, you may be liable for damages and even for a type of suit—unique to real estate—that calls for specific performance. The concept of specific performance is based on the fact that each property is different and that money damages may not adequately compensate the buyer who insists on purchasing your specific house.

Even if the buyers are agreeable to dropping their claims, remember that your real estate broker, having performed the services for which retained, may be entitled to full commission. Depending on circumstances, the broker may press a claim for the commission or may waive it in favor of your goodwill and the hope of future business.

If the buyer backs out with no adequate reason, you may be entitled to damages; and your broker may be entitled to a commission, for which you are liable. Your lawyer will know whether legal action is indicated. To avoid a lawsuit, the buyer often abandons the earnest money deposit. Sometimes that sum is then divided between seller and broker.

Occasionally, a transaction falls apart with no one at fault. Certain conditions in the contract may be impossible to fulfill; the buyer may fail to secure the mortgage loan; or you may be unable to provide marketable title. In such a case, the purchase contract may specify that the buyer is to receive full return of the deposit.

Delivering the Deed and Collecting Your Money

*W*hat does a typical settlement look like? In one city, buyers, sellers, attorneys, brokers and a paralegal from the lending institution may gather around a long table. In another area, there may not be a meeting at all; details are handled by mail through a special escrow company. In no aspect of real estate does local custom vary more.

Whatever the practice, however, the skeleton of the transaction remains the same:

- The seller proves marketable title.
- The buyer pays for the property.
- The seller delivers the deed.

If new financing is involved, settlement is complicated by the signing and delivery of a bond and mortgage or, in some states, a trust deed.

If you are unable to attend the closing, your lawyer may arrange for you to sign the deed ahead of time; this one act is your major contribution to the ceremonies. Just remember to leave the front-door keys also. If you give someone a power of attorney, authorizing them to act for you at the closing, that power is good only as long as you are alive. You may be asked, therefore, to leave a phone number where you can be reached at the time of closing, and the conversation will go something like this: "Hi there, how are you?" "Fine, thank you." It's just enough to prove you're still among the living.

187. Will we close on the exact date stated in the contract?

As soon as a firm mortgage commitment has been secured by the purchaser, the person in charge of the settlement can arrange a date suitable to all parties. Additional paperwork may be required, and several attorneys may need to dovetail their schedules; your moving plans and the buyers' must be considered.

If your contract stipulates a certain closing date and that day comes and goes, the contract is still in force. In most cases, the day specified is simply a target date. Only if time is made of the essence is it an "or else" item.

Except as it corresponds with your plans to move, there's no benefit to you in picking a particular day of the month—unless you will be paying off an FHA mortgage. Most lenders will charge you interest only until the exact date of the payoff, but HUD, the parent body of FHA, will charge interest for the whole present month. Pay off an FHA loan on June 1st, and you'll still owe interest for the whole month of June. If you're in that situation, you'd probably prefer to close toward the end of a month.

188. What should we do to prepare for closing?

You have called your utility companies to arrange for final readings of your meters. It may be practical to have the oil tank filled completely so that you will know how much you are leaving behind. You can pay this bill and then settle with the buyer at closing.

You have held your garage sale, notified the post office and magazine publishers, talked with the telephone company, secured a mover and finished your packing.

You have cleared out your safe-deposit box, stopped the newspaper, arranged babysitting for moving day and emptied the refrigerator.

You have packed a box of basics to take in your own car: medications, linens, flashlight, light bulbs, coffee pot and coffee, salt and sugar, towels, dishes, extension cords, a hammer and screwdriver, pots and silverware, cleaning cloths, soap, paper towels, broom and trash bags.

What next?

Plan on leaving your house in "broom-clean" condition: if not spotless, it should be neat, at least. Broom-clean condition assumes that piles of old newspapers have been removed, the refrigerator is clean, trash has been removed or left in a tidy fashion and floors have received one final sweeping.

189. What should I do if the buyers requests a last-minute walk-through?

This is a reasonable and prudent step for them, and they may have included a walk-through request in the contract. The buyer wants to check for newly broken windowpanes, make sure you are leaving the stove you promised and uncover any last-minute problems before closing, rather than afterwards. As usual, it is helpful if the buyer is accompanied by the broker, with your participation limited to a few cordial bits of information or advice about the property.

Make a last-minute check of the fine print on your purchase contract to see that you have kept your promises regarding items such as fireplace equipment, smoke alarms and playground equipment.

When you go to the closing, be sure to take all door keys and remote controls for your garage doors.

190. What items are adjusted at closing?

You and the buyers have a number of financial details to settle. Property taxes will undoubtedly be adjusted. In some areas, taxes are paid in advance. In this case, if you met your last bill, you have paid for the year ahead. If you close at, for example, the end of the fourth month, the buyers will receive a house with taxes paid for the year, and they should reimburse you for the eight months to come.

In other areas, property taxes are paid in arrears, as opposed to in advance. The bill for the current year will not be due for eight months. Because you have lived in the house for four months, you should credit a sum equaling four months' taxes to the new owner, who will later pay for the full year.

In the same way, you will adjust water or sewer charges.

If there are tenants, you should turn over any security deposits and advance rents to the new owner, who will return these monies to the tenants when they vacate the house.

If the buyers are assuming your mortgage, interest payments will be adjusted so that you pay for the days that you owned the house. The new owners will have to meet the next bill, which will cover the present month's interest.

Your current mortgage payments may include monthly charges for tax or insurance fees. Your lender sets up an escrow or reserve account for the purpose of collecting these funds for later disbursal. If the mortgage is being paid off rather than assumed, you will receive the balance of this account directly from the lender. Otherwise, the new owner will reimburse you for monies in this account, which remains with the mortgage.

You may be asked for a bill of sale on furniture or appliances being left with the property. The buyer pays for the full tank of oil you left behind; if costs have changed, custom dictates that you receive today's price.

The attorneys for both parties, or the persons in charge of the settlement session, agree on figures for all these adjustments and gradually fill out their closing statements.

191. What expenses will I have at closing?

Some closing costs are negotiable between seller and buyer, although the last minute is not the time for these negotiations. Other costs are yours and may include the following:

- *Liens and claims against your property*. Before the purchasers will take title, they usually insist that you clear up unpaid taxes, your present mortgage, home improvement loans, mechanics' liens, judgments and any other liens on record.
- *Special assessments*. In the absence of any other agreement, you may be expected to pay in one lump sum special charges levied against your area in the past few years for new sidewalks, street lighting or other improvements.
- *Transfer tax*. In some states or localities, a tax is due when property is transferred, and you may find a legal provision that this one expense must be paid by the seller.
- *Attorney or escrow agent*. You owe your own attorney's fees. Beyond that, the question of who pays for settlement services is usually established by local practice.
- *Survey, title insurance, termite inspection*. Again based on custom, the contract you signed dictates whether you or the buyer will pay.
- *Prepayment penalty*. You may owe a fee to the lender if you pay off your conventional loan before its due date. State laws have been whittling away at these charges, however.

192. What should I do if I'm taking back financing?

If you will be holding a first or second mortgage or a land contract yourself, the document can be drawn up by your attorney. If the buyer offers to pay for preparing the mortgage, be sure to have your own lawyer approve or amend it. In most states, the mortgage you will receive consists of two parts: a note or bond (personal promise to pay back the loan) and the mortgage or trust deed, which is a claim against the property if the promises made in the bond are not kept.

Just as the buyer is advised to put the deed on record immediately, so should you see that the mortgage is promptly entered into the public records. This will give you priority, ahead of later claims on the property, if there is trouble in the future.

If you are paying off a present mortgage, that fact, along with a certificate of satisfaction, should be filed in the public records at this time.

When you are in possession of the largest check you may ever have (it should be a certified check or money order, by the way), you are ready to turn over your property to the new owner. As the seller, you sign the deed. It may take one of several forms, depending on the situation, state law and local custom:

- A quitclaim deed simply transfers any rights you may have in the property.
- A special warranty deed (or bargain and sale deed with covenants) transfers your rights and promises that you have in no undisclosed way encumbered the property.
- A full warranty deed further guarantees the buyer's protection against claims raised by any other parties.

Because the transfer of title gives the new owner your rights in the real estate, you are called the grantor. Often, only the grantor signs the deed. Title to the property transfers at the moment you place the deed into the hands of the grantee.

"Signed, sealed and delivered" is the old phrase, and at the moment of physical delivery and acceptance of the deed, the property is no longer yours.

In most areas, you are expected to leave the house vacant on the day of closing. In some parts of the country, it's customary to allow you a few days after closing.

If you need to negotiate any time beyond that, the new owner may require a high rent, sometimes one that escalates the longer you remain—all intended to motivate you to move as soon as possible.

Chapter 24

*S*haring Proceeds with the IRS–Considering Your Options

*T*he sale of your home will be reported to the Internal Revenue Service (IRS) on a 1099 form similar to those you may have received that report interest and dividend payments. This procedure has been in effect since 1987.

Responsibility for submitting the report lies with the party in charge of the closing: title or escrow company, mortgage lender, seller's or buyer's attorney, real estate broker or even, if no one else files the report, the buyer. Your Social Security number must be included on the report, and you will probably be asked to furnish it at closing, along with your new address, so that you can be sent a copy of the 1099.

193. Must I report the sale even if I don't have any capital gain?

You'd better report it, to avoid trouble later.

Even if no tax is due on your profit, and even if you suffer a nondeductible loss, it is important that the sale be reported on your federal income tax return. If you ignore the matter, your return will not match the 1099 the IRS receives. Eventually, the matter will come back to haunt you, with irritating paperwork and correspondence at the very least.

You report the sale of your own primary residence on Form 2119. The sale of a vacation home or rental property is reported on Schedule D. For further information, you may want to call the IRS at 800-829-3676 and ask the agency to send you a free copy of Publication 523, "Tax Information on Selling Your Home." Professional assistance in preparing your tax return is usually required for the year in which you sell your home. If large sums or complicated matters are involved, it is wise to consult an accountant or a lawyer who specializes in tax planning before the sale.

Free help is available from the IRS itself, either by phone or in person. As income tax time approaches, IRS and tax specialists are increasingly busy; you will receive more thorough help if you seek it as early as possible.

Many states follow the federal regulations outlined below; your state may or may not offer the same special income tax treatment for homesellers.

Several favorable federal tax breaks are available for the treatment of profit realized on the sale of your main home, known to the IRS as your *principal residence*. In general, this is considered to be the place where you reside most of the time. It may be a mobile home or a houseboat, a cooperative or a condominium apartment. If you own one home but live in another that you rent, your principal residence is the rented house, and no special tax treatment would apply to the sale of the house you own.

194. What if I have a loss when I sell?

If you sell your own home (or a vacation home you don't rent out) at a loss, no deduction is allowed on your income tax return. You may not claim a capital loss. The rules, of course, are different for business or rental property, which qualifies for capital gain or loss treatment in the ordinary way, on Schedule D.

195. How do I calculate my capital gain?

The first step in figuring your profit is to determine your cost basis. To the original price of your home, add certain closing costs and the money you have spent on improvements over the years. Improvements are permanent additions to the value of your property; repairs and redecorating don't count. A new roof or furnace counts as an improvement; fixing the old one would be considered a repair and does not add to your cost basis.

Among improvements you might not think to add in at this point are—if you paid for them—fences, driveway paving (but not maintenance), wall-to-wall carpeting, permanent fixtures, new roof or furnace, finished basement or attic, new bath, new (not repaired) plumbing, new wiring, remodeling, new addition, insulation, storm windows and screens, and permanent landscaping.

If you did not buy your home, special provisions apply. If you built it, you may not include as part of cost basis the value of your labor or any friend's labor that you did not pay for. If you received the house as a gift, your cost basis is generally the giver's cost basis. If you inherited the house, you use a stepped-up basis, usually the value of the property when the former owner died.

Items you must subtract from cost basis include any losses you may have deducted on income tax returns for fire or other cause, money you received in return for easements, energy improvement credits you may have claimed or depreciation you may have claimed when all or part of your home was formerly used for a home office or as a rental.

Once you have your adjusted cost basis, subtract it from the selling price to arrive at your capital gain. You may also subtract legal costs of selling, real estate commissions, points or title insurance if you paid them yourselves, and some legal costs of buying, way back when.

When computing your profit (capital gain), the IRS is not interested in any mortgage you may have or pay off on the property. What counts is cost basis, sale price and costs of selling.

196. What special homesellers' tax breaks can I expect?

Two special tax treatments are available for the sale of your own home:

- Homeowners of any age must postpone tax on all or part of their profit if they purchase another main home within two years of selling the first one.
- Those aged 55 years and older at the time of sale may choose, once in a lifetime, to take up to $125,000 profit with no federal tax due ever.

If you buy another principal residence of equal or greater value within two years before or after you sell the first one (actually a four-year period around the sale), you do not owe tax immediately on your profit. Instead, your profit is subtracted from the cost basis of the next home. Here's how it works:

You buy Home A for $50,000 and sell it for $120,000. You promptly buy Home B for $150,000. The $70,000 profit you realized on the sale of A is not presently taxed. Instead, the cost basis of Home B is considered to be $150,000 minus that untaxed $70,000. Your cost basis on Home B will be $80,000.

Later, you sell Home B for $175,000. Subtracting your cost basis of $80,000 gives you taxable profit of $95,000. Looking at it another way, your profit on A was $70,000 and your profit on B was $25,000, giving you a combined profit of $95,000.

This process can be repeated indefinitely (not more than once every two years), piling up untaxed profits on a string of more expensive homes.

197. What should I do if my replacement home costs less than the one I sold?

You will defer tax on part of your profit and pay tax only on the remainder. Here's how this might look:

You bought Home A for $50,000 and sold it for $120,000. You then move to a smaller home costing $100,000. Tax on $50,000 of your profit is deferred. You will owe income tax now on the $20,000 of your profit that theoretically remained in your pocket once the dust had cleared.

These examples are merely skeletal and don't take into account any adjustments to cost basis and sales price.

198. I've rented out the downstairs apartment in my home. Do I get the tax break?

If you use part of your property for a farm, a home office, a rental apartment or other business property, your sale is treated, for tax purposes, as two separate transactions. The chance to defer taxes will apply to that percentage of the real estate considered to be your residence. The balance of your proceeds will be taxed as if you had sold business property.

If your home is rented out just before you sell it (particularly for a period exceeding one year), the house may have been converted to business property and may not qualify for the special rollover tax provisions on the sale of a residence. The law does allow a temporary period of rental simply for convenience, however, without jeopardizing the house's status as your residence.

Complex calculations apply to situations in which two homes are sold by a newly married couple, or when those recently separated replace one home with two. In each case, regulations are set up for the amount of profit on which tax may be deferred. Seek professional assistance for tax returns with any unusual conditions.

For homeowners of any age, then, and in almost every case, tax on the profit from the sale of one's home can be postponed indefinitely, probably not becoming due until one's last home is sold and no replacement home is purchased.

At that point, if you've turned age 55, you might sell your long-time home and use that $125,000 tax-free provision to cover the deferred taxes on profit from several houses back, so that you get off free in the end. Or if you own that last home until you die, your heirs receive the property with current valuation as their "stepped-up" cost basis. That makes death the ultimate tax shelter.

199. How does the one-time over-55 exclusion work?

This pleasant tax provision allows for a once-in-a-lifetime sale with profit up to $125,000 and with no federal tax due, ever. This treatment can also include the untaxed profits from previous homes, to a total of $125,000. You choose the time when you want to use this tax break. It's available whether or not you buy a replacement home.

You qualify if

- you have owned and occupied the property as your principal residence for at least three of the five years before the sale;
- you are age 55 years or older on the date the sale closes; and
- neither you nor your spouse, if you have one, has ever taken advantage of this exclusion before. The exclusion applies only once in a lifetime and only once to a couple.

If a married couple own the house, only one need meet the age, ownership and occupancy test for the sale to qualify. Problems arise, though, if either spouse (even one not officially listed as an owner) has used the exclusion previously. Even a nonowner spouse must join in the choice to use this tax break. Neither can ever use it again, nor could a new spouse of either one in a later marriage.

Two older persons contemplating marriage who intend to sell their homes and buy another should consider closing both sales before their wedding date. In that case, each would be entitled to claim a full $125,000 exclusion.

If part of your home has been used for rental or business, again you treat your sale as two separate transactions, applying the $125,000 exclusion to that fraction of your profit attributable to your own residence.

Different rules applied to a less generous, once-in-a-lifetime opportunity before July 26, 1978. Those who took advantage of the old provision may also have one turn at the new $125,000 exclusion.

It is possible to qualify for the exclusion, in some cases, even if it was a now-deceased spouse who owned and occupied the house for the required number of years.

You may accumulate the necessary three years' occupancy even with temporary absences during the five-year period. Rental for less than two years during the five-year period will not alter your eligibility. If you are in a state-licensed nursing home, you can count up to two years' residence there toward the three years needed in your own home.

If you change your mind and wish you hadn't used the $125,000 exclusion, or if you pay the tax and then decide to use the exclusion, you have a three-year period in which to amend your income tax return and make the change.

Although the law makes constant reference to the role of the spouse, who must join in choosing to use the exclusion, the opportunity is, of course, available to unmarried homeowners age 55 and older as well. Unmarried joint owners (brother and sister, for example, or unrelated persons) who sell their home may each use the full exclusion on his or her share of profit. This assumes, of course, that the house is the primary residence for both of them.

200. If I can't use special tax breaks, how is my profit taxed?

If you do not buy a replacement residence, and if you do not take the 55-and-older exclusion, you will owe income tax on the profit from the sale of real estate.

Capital Gains.   Your profit is classified as a short-term or long-term capital gain, depending on how long you have owned the house. At various times, Congress allowed you to disregard tax on 50 percent of your long-term capital gains, or 40 percent. In the mid-1990s, capital gains were simply taxed as ordinary income, though never at more than 28 percent.

Installment Treatment.   If you take back financing for all or part of the purchase price (hold a mortgage, with the buyer paying you monthly), you will owe tax on your profit year by year, as you collect it, unless that profit is covered by one of the homesellers' tax breaks. You could choose, instead, to pay the whole capital gains tax in the first year. Once you have chosen a certain treatment, however, you cannot go back and change your mind later.

201. Are there any special tax considerations about giving the house to my kids?

If you sell your home to your children or transfer title in any way that does not involve the open market, you have a transaction that may be ruled "not arm's length." Before you take any such action, discuss with an attorney the income or estate tax consequences. The IRS has definite ideas about the interest you might charge your children if you took back a mortgage from them.

The gift of one's homestead to a son or daughter may mean the elderly parent loses favorable property tax treatment, becomes liable for payment of state gift tax or faces an unexpected problem in the event of a child's divorce or bankruptcy. Once the child owns the house, the parent could no longer qualify for the $125,000 exclusion on its sale.

In certain circumstances, it is more prudent for children to wait to inherit property (with a stepped-up basis) than to receive it as a gift. The disposition of real estate should be considered in the wider framework of estate planning, and professional guidance is essential.

Index

A

Abatements, 33
Abstract, 105
Adding on vs. selling, 112-13
Adjustable-rate mortgage, 29, 66-69
    assumable with lender's
        approval, 155
    vocabulary of, 67-69
Adjustment period, 69
Adjustments, 167
Advertising, 125, 143, 179-80
Agency relationship, 8-9
Agent(s)
    buyers' brokers, 138
    commission, 138, 149, 153, 225-
      26
    discount brokers, 149, 153
    dismissing unsatisfactory, 144-
      45
    educational background of, 137
    fiduciary duties owed to seller,
      142-45
    finding and working with, 14-
      20, 130-32, 135-36
    guaranteed sale and, 139-40
    legal obligations to seller's, 15,
      16-17
    licensing commission for, 145
    protection of interests and, 10-
      11
    presale home preparation
      suggestions from, 174
    price recommendation of, 136
    selection criteria, 129-30, 134-
      35, 139
    seller's brokers, 142-45
    services provided by, 17-20,
      124-27
    types of, 7-8, 127-29, 132-34
Agreement to buy and sell, 80

Alimony, 97, 98, 99
American Association of Retired
    Persons (AARP), 114-15
American Society of Home
    Inspectors, 55
Amortization, 5, 67
Amortization schedule, 26-27
Annual percentage rate, 64-65
Application fee, 100
Appraisal, 100, 166, 169, 171
    problems with, 224-25
Asbestos, 55
Assessments, 167, 231
Assets, and loan application process,
    97-98
Assumable mortgages, 75-76, 83,
    154-55, 207-9, 230
    advantages of, 207-8
    bank approval for, 76
    drawbacks, 208
    home price and, 165-67
    VA loans and, 73, 154-55, 208
    with approval, 209
Attorneys, 140-41
    approval of contract, 200-201
    legal fees and, 167, 231

B

Balloon mortgage, 78-79
Bankruptcy, 99, 100
Bank standards, 209-10
Bargain and sale deed, 106, 232
Bargains, 45-49
Basement, 38, 53-54, 177
Bathrooms, 177
Bedrooms, 37, 177
Before-closing checklist, 107
Better business bureau, 145
Bill of sale, 106
Binder, 86-87